# Science Bridge

Yoshinobu Nozaki Kazuko Matsumoto Alastair Graham-Marr

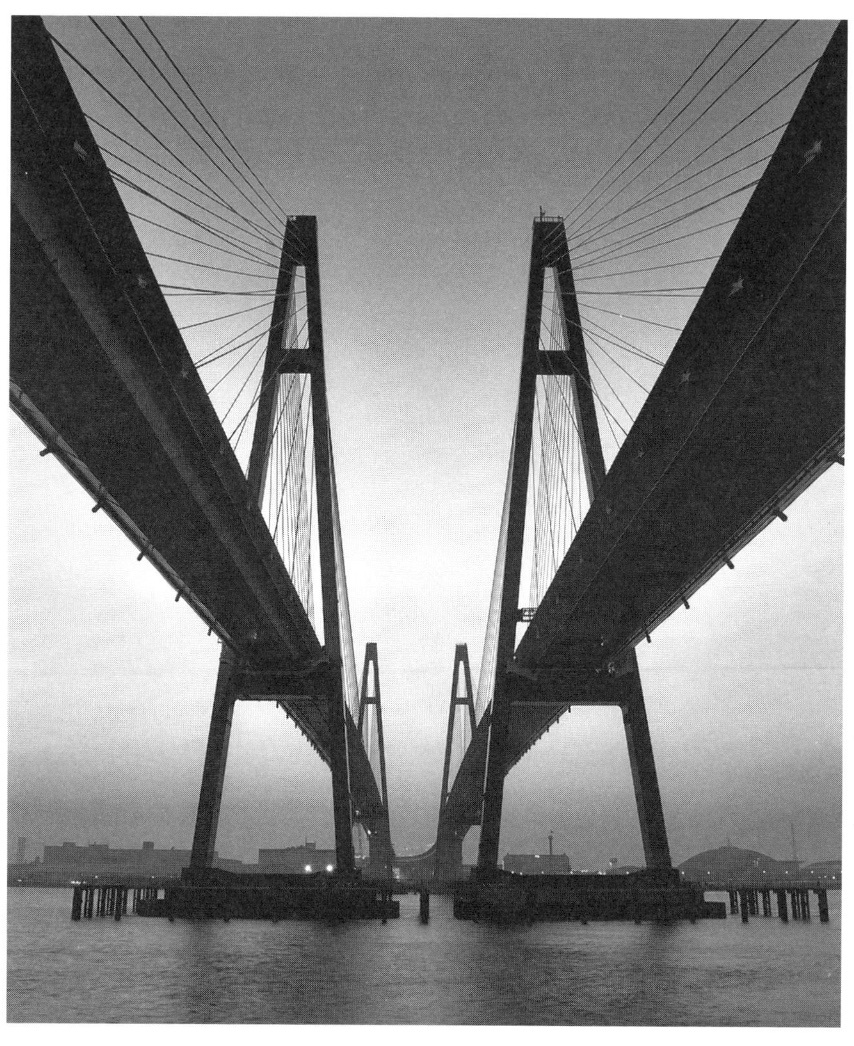

KINSEIDO

**Kinseido Publishing Co., Ltd.**
3-21 Kanda Jimbo-cho, Chiyoda-ku,
Tokyo 101-0051, Japan



First published 2024 by Kinseido Publishing Co., Ltd.

Cover design: Takayuki Minegishi
Text design: DAITECH co., ltd.
Editorial support: C-leps Co., Ltd.

## 音声ファイル無料ダウンロード

https://www.kinsei-do.co.jp/download/4203

**この教科書で DL 00 の表示がある箇所の音声は、上記 URL または QR コードにて無料でダウンロードできます。自習用音声としてご活用ください。**

- ▶ PC からのダウンロードをお勧めします。スマートフォンなどでダウンロードされる場合は、**ダウンロード前に「解凍アプリ」をインストール**してください。
- ▶ URL は、**検索ボックスではなくアドレスバー（URL 表示覧）**に入力してください。
- ▶ お使いのネットワーク環境によっては、ダウンロードできない場合があります。

CD 00　左記の表示がある箇所の音声は、教室用 CD（Class Audio CD）に収録されています。

# はしがき

本書 *Science Bridge* は、幅広い年齢層を対象とするオンライン科学ニュースサイト Science News Explores を題材にした総合英語教材です。一流科学ジャーナリストが執筆する記事は、質の高さをそのままに平易な英語で記されており、トピックの面白さと相俟って読者を無理なく英文科学記事の世界に導きます。歯切れよい簡潔な文体は、英語学習者の見本ともなるでしょう。

Science News Explores には、Humans, Space, Life などを含む 9 つのメインカテゴリーのもとに、Health & Medicine, Planets, Ecosystem といった 15 を超えるサブカテゴリーが配置されています。理系・文系の区別なく興味を持っていただけるように、本書は同サイトのカテゴリーを踏まえ、分野の偏りなく厳選した 15 のトピックを集めて編集いたしました。生態系のバランスを崩す人工光の問題（Unit 1 Artificial Light on the Sea）、母親の声に注意を向けなくなる思春期の謎を解明する脳科学研究（Unit 2 Tuning Out Mom's Voice?）、産業への活用が期待される生きた皮膚で覆われた指型ロボットの誕生（Unit 6 Robotic Finger）、頻発する山火事が拍車をかける大気汚染（Unit 9 Wildfire and Air Pollution）、生活習慣のひとつである歯磨きに着目したユニークなアレルギー治療法（Unit 11 Might Toothpaste Cure Allergies?）、小惑星に探査機をぶつけて軌道を変えることで他の天体との衝突から地球を守る可能性を一気に高めた NASA の壮大な実験（Unit 12 NASA's DART Spacecraft）などが具体例です。

各ユニットは 7 ページ構成です。記事の紹介を兼ねた日本語の紹介文から始まり、記事内の単語に目を慣らしておく予備的ドリル **Word Choice** が続きます。準備が整ったところで **Reading** に進み、2 つのパートに分けて編集された記事を読みます。難解な表現や用語は含まれておらず、スムーズな読解を手助けする側注や ***Further Notes*** が添えてあるので、科学記事を初めて読む場合でも心配はいりません。記事を楽しんだら ***Exercises*** に挑戦です。KEY PHRASES では語句レベルの運用力を、IN-DEPTH REVIEW では読解力をそれぞれチェックしてみましょう。次のページの **Summary** は、記事の流れがつかめているかどうかを確認する問題です。問題に答える過程は、各パートの内容を整理し、要約をする作業でもあります。正解が導けたかどうかの確認には音声が利用可能で、リスニング力も鍛えられます。内容がしっかり頭に入ったところで、記事で扱われている語法に目を転じます。英作文の練習として ***Writing Strategy*** を用意しました。取り組みやすい並べ替えスタイルを採用してあります。文法事項を押さえながら日本語の意味に合うように英作文して下さい。続く ***Clue to Usage*** は、重要な文法事項や構文に注意を促すだけでなく、多彩な言い換え表現の紹介や語（句）がもつ微妙なニュアンスの解説などにも目配りしてあります。分量的に重くならないよう、テーマは各ユニットにつき 2 つに絞り込んであります。次に置かれた ***Approaching the Contents*** は、ユニットの締め括りとして記事の要点をもう一度確認するタスクです。リスニングと内容把握の要素を組み合わせた複合的練習問題に取り組むことで、ユニットの内容を十分に消化していただきます。最終ページの **Over to you!** は、記事に関連するエッセイやコラム、データにアレンジを加えて問題に編集したコーナーで、アクティブラーニングへの挑戦を促すパートです。関連データの一部となる図や表の空欄を補充してデータを完成させ、FAQs のスタイルを模した質問文と回答文を読み取りながら記事の理解を深めるなど、複数のパターンを提示しました。この部分は、グループディスカッションや自主リサーチなど、教室での発展学習のヒントにもなるものと期待しています。

このように本書は、素材である Science News Explores の魅力に親しみながら英語力向上が図れるよう工夫したテキストを目指しています。*Science Bridge* のタイトルのとおり、本書との出会いが、日々の生活の場と科学の世界との橋渡しの一助となれば幸いです。

金星堂編集部の皆様には長期間にわたって貴重な助言と温かい励ましをいただきました。厚くお礼を申し上げます。

2024 年 3 月　編著者一同

# Science Bridge

Contents

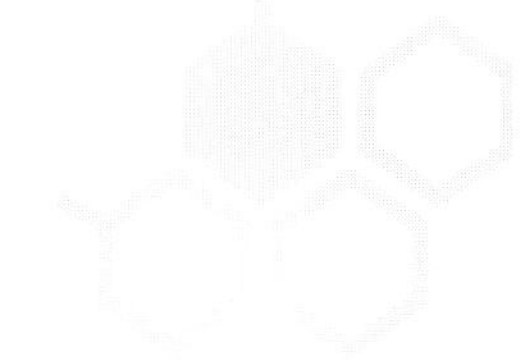

# Unit 1

# Artificial Light on the Sea

## 生態系を脅かす明るい夜

明かりに邪魔されず天体観測ができる場所を探せるアプリを知っていますか。このアプリの普及を後押ししているのは深刻化する光害問題です。過度な明るさによる人体や生態系への被害が、世界で報告されています。アプリのマップに浮かぶ黄色やオレンジは、環境破壊への警告灯でもあるのです。

## Word Choice

**日本語の意味に合うように a ～ f から適切な語を選びましょう。ただし、選択肢には解答と関係のないものもあります。**

Part 1

| | | |
|---|---|---|
| **1.** | 世界的インフレについて警鐘を鳴らす | send a wake-up call about (　　　　) inflation |
| **2.** | 海岸浸食の現地調査を行う | conduct an on-site survey for some (　　　　) erosion |
| **3.** | 沖合の島に向かうボート旅行を予約する | book a boat trip to (　　　　) islands |
| **4.** | AI 技術を運転に適用する | apply (　　　　) intelligence technology to driving |
| **5.** | 海洋生物の多様性を確保する | ensure a diversity of (　　　　) life |

**a.** artificial　**b.** coastal　**c.** global　**d.** marine　**e.** offshore　**f.** southern

Part 2

| | | |
|---|---|---|
| **1.** | 大気中の二酸化炭素を減らす | reduce carbon dioxide in the (　　　　) |
| **2.** | 研究室に新規採用された同僚を歓迎する | welcome a newly employed (　　　　) in the laboratory |
| **3.** | 恐竜絶滅の決定的要因を突き止める | pinpoint a decisive (　　　　) in the extinction of dinosaurs |
| **4.** | 野生動物保護区での被食・捕食関係を調べる | study the prey-(　　　　) relationships in a wildlife reserve |
| **5.** | 映画監督からの合図を待つ | wait for a (　　　　) from the film director |

**a.** atmosphere　**b.** colleague　**c.** confuse　**d.** cue　**e.** factor　**f.** predator

DL 02 CD1-02 ~ CD1-10

# Reading

## Night lights make even the seas bright

### Part 1

Not even the sea is safe from the glare of humans' light at night. Researchers published the first global atlas of ocean light pollution. It shows large chunks of the sea lit up at night. And that risks confusing or disrupting the behaviors of sea life.

Coastal cities cast haloes of light that stretch over the ocean. So do offshore oil rigs and other structures. In many places, the glow is powerful enough to penetrate deep into coastal waters. And that light risks changing behaviors of the creatures that live there.

Artificial lights are known to affect land dwellers. Night lighting can prevent plant pollination and foil fireflies' flashes. They even make it harder for sparrows to fight off West Nile virus. Bright lights near shores can spread the glow out to sea.

Tim Smyth led a research team to assess where in the water this glow is strongest. Smyth is a marine biogeochemist. That means he studies how life in the oceans interacts with the environment using biology, chemistry and geology. He works at Plymouth Marine Laboratory on the southern coast of England.

Notes

glare まぶしい輝き
chunk 大きな塊
risks confusing or disrupting ～ ～を混乱させたり乱したりする恐れがある
haloes of light 丸い光の輪
oil rig 石油掘削装置
coastal water 沿岸水域
dweller 居住者、居住動物
pollination 授粉
foil fireflies' flash 蛍の発光を妨げる
fight off ～ ～を撃退する
geology 地質学

### Part 2

Smyth and his colleagues started with a world atlas of artificial night-sky brightness that had been created in 2016. Then they added data on the ocean and atmosphere. Some data came from shipboard measurements of artificial light in the water. Others came from satellite images that estimate how clear the water is. Particles in the water, such as sediment and tiny floating plants and animals, can affect how far downward light travels. These factors vary from place to place and may change with the seasons. The team also used computers to simulate how different wavelengths of light move through water.

Next, they wanted to know how that underwater light

particle 微粒子ないし小片
sediment 沈殿物
wavelength 波長

might affect animals. Not all species will be equally sensitive. The team focused on copepods. These common shrimplike creatures are a key part of many ocean food webs. Like other tiny zooplankton, copepods use light as a cue to plunge en masse to the dark deep, seeking safety from surface predators. Normally they use the sun or the winter moon as their cue. Too much artificial light can mess up their usual patterns.

copepod カイアシ

zooplankton 動物性プランクトン
cue 合図
plunge 飛び込む
en masse 集団で、一斉に

mess up ~ ~をめちゃくちゃにする

Light pollution is strongest in the top meter (about three feet) of the water. Here, artificial light can be intense enough to confuse the copepods. Nearly 2 million square kilometers (770,000 square miles) of ocean get such intense night light. That's an area roughly the size of Mexico.

square kilometer 平方キロメートル

Farther down, the light gets weaker. But even 20 meters (65 feet) deep, it's still bright enough to bother copepods across 840,000 square kilometers (325,000 square miles) of ocean.

The team described its findings December 13 in *Elementa: Science of the Anthropocene.*

(456 words)

## *Further Notes*

ℓ.12 **West Nile virus** 1937 年ウガンダの West Nile 地方の発熱患者から発見されたウイルス。アメリカ、西アジア、中央アジア、中東、ヨーロッパなど広範囲に分布。鳥と蚊の間に感染サイクルが形成され、主に蚊を介してヒトに感染し、ウエストナイル熱や脳炎を引き起こす。野鳥への被害も大きく、多数の感染が確認されているが、通常、スズメは発症せずにウイルスを保有している。

ℓ.18 **Plymouth Marine Laboratory** イギリスのプリマス（イングランド南西部デヴォン州の港湾都市）に設立された海洋研究所。1988 年の設立以来、海洋学の領域にとどまらず地球規模での環境問題全般を対象に調査・研究を実施している。マイクロプラスチックが海洋生物に与える影響の研究はその一例。

ℓ.47 ***Elementa: Science of the Anthropocene*** 学際的なオープンアクセスのオンライン学術専門誌。 ＊ Anthropocene「人新世（じんしんせい／ひとしんせい）」：ノーベル化学賞受賞者のパウル・クルッツェンが 2000 年に考案した「人類の時代」という意味の新しい時代区分。人類が地球の生態系や大気に多大な影響を与えるようになった時代、という意味で、現在の完新世の次の地質区分を表す。

## Exercises

KEY PHRASES

**(　　) に適切な語句を語群から選び英文を完成させましょう。ただし、必要に応じて語形は変えること。**

1. The entrance ceremony last April (　　　　　　　　　) a speech made by the president.
2. The budget provided by the company will (　　　　　　　　　) project to project.
3. The vaccine (　　　　　　　　　) another drug and resulted in a deadly side effect.
4. We need to stop (　　　　　　　　　) unimportant details or we'll never move the discussion forward.
5. Some insects succeed in (　　　　　　　　　) their predators by emitting poisonous chemicals.

| fight off | focus on | interact with | start with | vary from |
|---|---|---|---|---|

IN-DEPTH REVIEW

**本文の内容に合うようにa～cから(　　)に適切な語(句)を選びましょう。**

t 1

1. One effect of artificial light is that it can be (　　　　) to some marine creatures.
   a. beneficial　　b. stimulating　　c. stressful
2. Tim Smyth and his teammates aimed to identify (　　　　).
   a. the largest chunk of the sea lit up at night
   b. the brightest place in the water
   c. the interactions among life in the ocean

t 2

1. (　　　　) affect the depth to which light can penetrate water.
   a. The shipboard measurements　　b. The particles in the air
   c. Some small sea organisms can
2. The researchers used (　　　　) of copepods to conduct their study.
   a. the light sensitivity　　b. the physical strength
   c. the popularity as the predator

DL 03 CD1-11

## Summary

**以下の a ～ d を本文に出てきた順番に合うように並べ替え、それぞれの Part の要約文を作りましょう。最後に音声を聞いて確認しましょう。**

Part 1

[ ] → [ ] → [ ] → [ ]

a. It has long been known that artificial night light poses a major threat to land animals.

b. For the first time, researchers surveyed ocean light pollution caused by humans on a global scale.

c. Powerful light emitted from coastal cities or offshore structures such as oil rigs spreads far out to sea.

d. Researchers examined where in the sea the glow of light is strongest.

Part 2

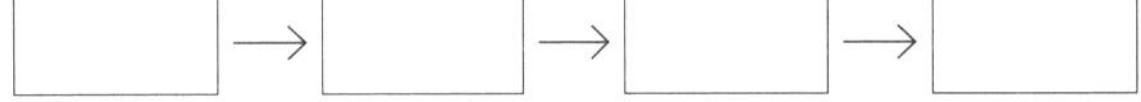

a. For example, they focused on copepods that make up an important part of ocean food webs.

b. Near the surface of the sea, copepods' behavior can be confused by strong artificial light to a great degree.

c. Using the data collected from shipboard measurements as well as satellite images, scientists analyzed how artificial light could interfere with sea creatures.

d. Copepods normally depend on natural light from the sun or the moon in order to seek safety from predators.

## Writing Strategy

**日本語の意味に合うように [　　] 内の語を並べ替え、英文を完成させましょう。**

1. 人工の光がどのように海洋生物の正常な行動に影響を与えるのかを知るために、研究者たちはデータを集めた。

   Researchers collected data to decide [ *artificial* / *behavior* / *can* / *how* / *light* / *normal* / *affect* ] of sea creatures.

   ______________________________________________

2. 「すべての種が光の輝きに等しく敏感だ、というわけではない」と、その科学者は言った。

   "[ *all* / *are* / *equally* / *not* / *sensitive* / *species* / *to* ] the glow of light," said the scientist.

   ______________________________________________

## Clue to Usage

### 倒置・部分否定

So do offshore oil rigs ... (ℓ. 6) は、前の文の cast haloes of light を So で受けて文頭に出したために、後ろの主語と動詞の語順が入れ替わった倒置の代表的な文例。Not all species ... (ℓ. 31) は、部分否定であることを明確にするために、このように Not で書き出すのが普通とされる。

### 間接疑問文

assess where ... this glow is strongest. (ℓ. 14) のほかにも、affect how far downward light travels (ℓ. 25) など、このユニットにはいくつか間接疑問文の文例がある。Where is this glow strongest? という疑問文を動詞 assess の目的語 (名詞節) として別の文中に取り込むと、クエスチョンマークは消え語順もS+Vに代わる、というルールで使うことができる。

ex) Who is she ? → I don't know who she is.

## Approaching the Contents

**質問文の下線部分を書き取り、解答を a ～ d から選びましょう。**

1 Q: Does bright light ______________________________ ?

a. Not in the least. They can hide deep in the forest.
b. The truth is that land animals are also threatened like sea creatures.
c. The brighter the light becomes, the safer the animals are.
d. That's right. Usually, they are stronger than fish.

2 Q: Why do copepods ______________________________ ?

a. Because they are not so sensitive to sunlight.
b. To avoid assault by predators.
c. The reason is that they are an essential part of food webs.
d. In fact, they need to hunt for tiny plankton.

# Over to you!

**以下の表では、光害の影響をまとめています。1～7に適切な語（句）を語群から選び、表中の英文を完成させましょう。ただし、必要に応じて語形は変えること。**

| | |
|---|---|
| animal | Artificial light damages the Earth's daily light and dark rhythm that (1. ) animal life-sustaining behaviors such as reproduction, sleep, and protection from predators. |
| human | An increased amount of light at night is likely to (2. ) melatonin production, which results in sleep disorders, fatigue, headaches, stress and other health problems. |
| ecosystem | Artificial light can cause fatal damage to insects. Declining insect populations negatively impact all species that (3. ) on insects for food or pollination. |
| driving | Glare (4. ) drivers at a higher risk of being unable to see pedestrians and obstacles on the road. Also, excessive light can lead the drivers to (5. ) traffic lights and signs. |
| energy | According to the survey in 2022, in the U.S. alone, outdoor lighting (6. ) about 380 TWh* every year. That's enough to power 35 million homes for one year. * TWh = terawatt hour |
| others | Our ancestors experienced a night sky that (7. ) science, religion, philosophy, and art. Millions of children across the globe will never know the wonder of the Milky Way. |

consume　inspire　lower　overlook　put　regulate　rely

# Unit 2

# Tuning Out Mom's Voice?

## お母さんの言うことが聞こえないのは脳のせい？

「ちゃんと聞いているの?!」一母親に叱られた覚えはありませんか？ 幼い頃には特別な地位にあった母親の声に、思春期になると興味を示さなくなることが立証されました。科学的には身体の成長に伴う脳の変化という現象にすぎませんが、母親の心中は複雑かもしれません。

## Word Choice

**日本語の意味に合うように a ～ f から適切な語を選びましょう。ただし、選択肢には解答と関係のないものもあります。**

1

| | | |
|---|---|---|
| **1.** | かなり英語を使いこなす | have a (　　　　) good command of English |
| **2.** | 脳の特定領野を調べる | examine a particular (　　　　) of the brain |
| **3.** | 彼女の態度の微妙な変化に気付く | (　　　　) a subtle change in her attitude |
| **4.** | ようやく青年期を通過する | finally pass through (　　　　) |
| **5.** | 新生活への移行を経験する | experience a (　　　　) into a new life |

**a.** adolescence　**b.** detect　**c.** fairly　**d.** opposite　**e.** region　**f.** transition

2

| | | |
|---|---|---|
| **1.** | その本は買う価値があるとみなす | regard the book as (　　　　) of purchasing |
| **2.** | その傾向を不安定な社会の反映と考える | consider the trend to be a (　　　　) of the unstable society |
| **3.** | 時間をかけて人間として成長する | (　　　　) as a person over the years |
| **4.** | 母親の出産時死亡率を測定する | monitor the rate of the (　　　　) death in childbirth |
| **5.** | 逃した機会を悔やむ | regret the (　　　　) opportunities |

**a.** biological　**b.** maternal　**c.** mature　**d.** missed　**e.** reflection　**f.** worthy

## Reading

### *Why teens can't help tuning out mom's voice*

Part 1

Do you sometimes ignore your mom while chatting with friends? If you're a teen, that's fairly common. And new research may explain why so many adolescents tune out their mom's voice.

Young kids' brains are very tuned in to their mothers' voices, science has shown. But as kids morph into teens, everything changes. Teenagers' brains are now more tuned in to strangers' voices than to their own moms', new research shows. "Adolescents have this whole other class of sounds and voices that they need to tune into," explains Daniel Abrams. He's a neuroscientist at Stanford University School of Medicine in California. He and his team shared their findings on April 28 in the *Journal of Neuroscience*.

The researchers scanned the brains of 7- to 16-year-olds as they listened to things said by their mothers or by unfamiliar women. The words were pure gibberish: teebudieshawlt, keebudieshawlt and peebudieshawlt. Using such nonsense words allowed the scientists to study voices on their own, not what they were saying. As the kids listened, certain parts of their brains became active. This was especially true in brain regions that help us to detect rewards and pay attention.

Abrams and his colleagues already knew that younger kids' brains respond more strongly to their mom's voice than to a stranger's. "In adolescence, we show the exact opposite of that," Abrams says. For teens, these brain regions respond more to unfamiliar voices than to their mom's. This shift in what voice piques interest most seems to happen between ages 13 and 14. That's when teenagers are in the midst of puberty, a roughly decade-long transition into adulthood.

Notes

adolescent 思春期の若者
tune out ~ ~を無視する
tune in to ~ ~に耳を傾ける
morph into ~ ~に姿を変える
class of ~ ~の類
tune into ~ ~に注意を払う
neuroscientist 神経科学者
gibberish でたらめ
on their own それ自身
brain region 脳の領野
reward 報酬
piques （興味を）かきたてる
puberty 思春期
adulthood 成人期

Part 2

These areas in the adolescent brain don't stop responding

to mom, Abrams says. It's just that unfamiliar voices become more rewarding and worthy of attention. Here's why: As kids grow up, they expand their social connections way beyond their family. So their brains need to begin paying more attention to that wider world. That's exactly as it should be, Abrams adds. "What we're seeing here is just purely a reflection of this."

But mothers' voices still have a special power, especially in times of stress, as one 2011 study on girls showed. Levels of stress hormones dropped when these stressed-out girls heard their moms' voices on the phone. The same wasn't true for texts from the moms.

The brain seems to adapt to new needs that come with adolescence. "As we mature, our survival depends less and less on maternal support," says Leslie Seltzer. She's a biological anthropologist at the University of Wisconsin–Madison. She was part of the team that carried out that 2011 study. Instead, she says, we rely more and more on our peers — friends and others closer to our own age.

So while both teens and their parents may sometimes feel frustrated by missed messages, that's okay, Abrams says. "This is the way the brain is wired, and there's a good reason for it."

(487 words)

rewarding 利益や報酬がある

way beyond ～ ～をはるかに超えて

stressed-out ストレスを抱えた

come with ～ ～と共に生じる

biological anthropologist 生物人類学者

missed message 聞き落とされたメッセージ

the way the brain is wired 脳の回線のありよう

*Further Notes*

ℓ.11 **Stanford University School of Medicine** スタンフォード大学医学部。1858 年に設立されたパシフィック大学医学部が前身。1885 年にスタンフォード大学が設立されると、1908 年に同大学へと統合された。

ℓ.13 ***Journal of Neuroscience*** 北米神経科学学会が発行している週刊学術誌。神経科学分野でのトップジャーナルとして高い評価を得ている。

ℓ.45 **University of Wisconsin-Madison** ウィスコンシン大学マディソン校。ウィスコンシン州マディソンに本部を置くアメリカ合衆国の名門州立大学。1848 年設立。

## Exercises

KEY PHRASES

(　　) に適切な語句を語群から選び英文を完成させましょう。ただし、必要に応じて語形は変えること。

1. (　　　　　　　　) her doctor's advice led to her ruining her health.
2. The researchers expected the microbe to (　　　　　　　　) moisture.
3. Some refugees have serious difficulties in (　　　　　　　　) a new environment.
4. We need to respect the knowledge and experiences that (　　　　　　　　) age.
5. To get accurate data, we will (　　　　　　　　) pre- and post-surveys of the experiment.

| adapt to | carry out | come with | respond to | tune out |
|---|---|---|---|---|

IN-DEPTH REVIEW

本文の内容に合うようにa～cから(　　)に適切な語句を選びましょう。

Part 1

1. Daniel Abram and his colleagues obtained the results by (　　　　).
   a. asking their mothers to speak meaningless words
   b. publishing the *Journal of Neuroscience*
   c. scanning the brains of young kids
2. Mom's voices (　　　　) early teenagers.
   a. become less appealing to　　b. increase the impact on
   c. sound more demanding to

Part 2

1. According to the study on the stressed girls, (　　　　) their stress hormone levels.
   a. a call from their mothers reduced
   b. the voices of their mothers maintained
   c. email from their mothers raised
2. According to Abram, teens can't help ignoring their mothers' voice because (　　　　).
   a. their brains are programmed to tune in to unfamiliar voices.
   b. they have already been frustrated by miscommunication with them
   c. they have started to depend more on paternal support

DL 06 CD1-21

## Summary

**以下の a ～ d を本文に出てきた順番に合うように並べ替え、それぞれの Part の要約文を作りましょう。最後に音声を聞いて確認しましょう。**

t 1

a. Scientists chose some nonsense words and let teenagers listen to them in order to examine their responses.

b. It is common for teenagers to tune out their mom's voice while talking to their friends.

c. When teenagers reach puberty, their brains become more sensitive to unfamiliar voices than to their mother's.

d. When the kids listened to such meaningless words, some particular regions of their brains became active.

t 2

☐ → ☐ → ☐ → ☐

a. As kids grow up, the range of their social connections necessarily becomes larger.

b. The brain starts to be wired in a new way with adolescence, and for a good reason.

c. As we mature, we will rely less on moms' influence than that of our peers, such as close friends.

d. Kids may seem to ignore maternal support, but moms' voices still maintain their healing power.

## Writing Strategy

**日本語の意味に合うように [　　] 内の語を並べ替え、英文を完成させましょう。**

1. 子供たちは、それが当然の姿だが、身近な友人たちに、より多くの注意を向けた。
Kids paid more attention to [ *as* / *be* / *close* / *friends,* / *it* / *should* / *their* ].

______________________________

2. どんな本が子供たちの関心を引くかは、年齢次第で大きな差がある。
The [ *attention* / *book* / *difference* / *draws* / *in* / *kids'* / *what* ] is great depending on their ages.

______________________________

## Clue to Usage

### whatの用例

what they are saying (ℓ. 19)「彼らの言っていること」や、what we're seeing (ℓ. 36)「私たちの見ているもの」のwhat は普通の関係代名詞だが、This shift in what voice piques interest most seems to happen ... (ℓ. 26) にあるwhatは読み取りが難しい。文全体の動詞はseemsなので、This shift ... most の節の部分が主語になる。鍵になる単語はpiques (動詞 = excite / arouse の意味) で、piques interest で「興味をそそる」と解釈できる。このwhatを関係代名詞と考えると意味が通らないが、後に名詞がつく疑問詞である疑問形容詞と考えると意味が通る。したがって「どんな声がいちばん興味をそそるか、そこの変化が…」と訳すことができる。

### asの用例

本文には As kids grow up (ℓ. 32) など、「時」を表すas「～するとき／～につれて」の用例がいくつもあるが、That's exactly as it should be (ℓ. 35) のas は Leave the book as it is.や、When in Rome, do as the Romans do.のasと同じく、「～のように」と「様態」を表す使い方である。さらにこの文にはshouldがあるため、文全体としては「まさにそれが当然あるべき姿なのだ」と訳すことができる。

ex) Make sure that everything is as it should be.「万事、しかるべき形になるよう気をつけてね」

## Approaching the Contents

**質問文の下線部分を書き取り、解答をａ～ｄから選びましょう。**

Part 1

Q: When are kids likely to ________________________________?

a. Immediately after they pay attention to rewards.
b. Before teenagers reach the age of puberty.
c. When they gradually develop into teens.
d. When their brain becomes inactive.

Part 2

Q: What will happen when kids ________________________________?

a. They become frustrated by missed support from their mother.
b. They decide not to continue responding to their mother.
c. They feel it necessary to pay more attention to the outer world.
d. They can survive stressful days all by themselves.

# Over to you!

1～4は脳に関するFAQです。質問に対する回答を(a)～(d)から選びましょう。また、[　　]に適切な語をKeywordsから選び、(a)～(d)の英文を完成させましょう。

## FAQs

1. How much does the brain weigh? (　　)
2. How does the brain control our body temperature? (　　)
3. Does the brain go to sleep when we do? (　　)
4. As the brain ages, do creativity and wisdom decline? (　　)

## Answers

**Keywords** 1. ability / 2. asleep / 3. lifetime / 4. thermostat

(a) When we sleep, we have an active brain, and dreams happen. The difference between awake and [　　　] is determined by which brain systems are activated at some point. Some brain chemicals work on different nerve cells in the brain, telling the brain to go to sleep and communicating which parts will stay active during our sleep.

(b) They do not decline over years. It's true that the brain indeed shrinks in volume, and blood flow decreases as we get older, but declines in thinking and memory are not inevitable. The brain can learn new things throughout our [　　　].

(c) The brain controls body temperature just like a [　　　]. The brain knows what temperature our body should be, and if our body is too hot, the brain tells us to sweat. If we are too cold, it makes us tremble.

(d) The human brain weighs 400g at birth. It's up to about 900g by elementary school age and eventually weighs 1300-1400g as an adult. The adult human brain has a size comparable to a grapefruit, shaped similar to a walnut, and a pinkish-gray color. The brain size of male humans is about 10% larger than that of females. However, differences in male and female brain size do not mean differences in mental [　　　].

# Unit 3 Smart Clothing

## 先端技術をまとう

最先端の科学を身近に感じさせてくれるもの、そのひとつは衣服です。例えば、軽くて暖かいインナーウエア。たった一枚の薄い布地で、重ね着したときと同じ暖かさを生み出すため、メーカーは人体の発熱、発汗の仕組みを解明し、体温を有効活用した次世代繊維の開発に励んでいます。

## Word Choice

**日本語の意味に合うように a ～ f から適切な語を選びましょう。ただし、選択肢には解答と関係のないものもあります。**

*Part 1*

| | | |
|---|---|---|
| **1.** | 通信販売の衣料ビジネスを始める | launch a mail-order (　　　　) business |
| **2.** | ハンドルをしっかり握る | (　　　　) the wheel tightly |
| **3.** | でこぼこの地面を走る | run on (　　　　) ground |
| **4.** | いくつかの有機化合物を合成する | synthesize some organic (　　　　) |
| **5.** | 食物から栄養を吸収する | (　　　　) nutrients from food |

**a.** absorb　**b.** apparel　**c.** compounds　**d.** grip　**e.** pores　**f.** uneven

*Part 2*

| | | |
|---|---|---|
| **1.** | 速乾性の布地を開発する | develop a quick-drying (　　　　) |
| **2.** | 高い利益を生むために休みなく働く | work round the clock to (　　　　) a high profit |
| **3.** | 二国間の貿易摩擦を最小限にする | minimize the trade (　　　　) between the two countries |
| **4.** | 大手小売チェーン店に投資する | invest in a large (　　　　) chain |
| **5.** | 最先端の研究所として評判を得る | gain a reputation for a cutting-edge (　　　　) |

**a.** fabric　**b.** friction　**c.** generate　**d.** lab　**e.** sole　**f.** retail

DL 08 CD1-23 ~ CD1-29

## Reading

### *Let's learn about the future of smart clothing*

*Part 1*

Our clothes do a lot for us. They keep us warm in the winter or cool while we're working out. They let us dress to impress or comfortably veg out on the couch. They let each of us express our unique sense of style. But some researchers think our clothes could be doing even more. Those scientists and engineers are dreaming up new ways to make clothes safer, comfier, or just more convenient.

Some ideas for new apparel aim to protect people from harm. One new shoe design, for example, features pop-out spikes on the sole that grip the ground. This could help people keep their footing on slippery or uneven terrain. A new fabric coating, meanwhile, could absorb and neutralize some chemical weapons. That coating is made from a metal-organic framework that snags and breaks down harmful compounds. It could offer a lightweight shield to people in war-torn countries.

Not all advanced attire is designed to save lives. Some could just make clothes more comfortable. One day, for instance, you may not need to layer up to stay warm. Fabric embedded with nanowires could reflect your body heat back onto your skin. Electric current humming through those metal threads could provide warmth, too. This may be especially useful for hikers, soldiers, or others working in super cold conditions.

On the flip side, another new fabric traps very little body heat. Tiny pores in this material are just the right size to block visible light waves — so the material isn't see-through — but let infrared waves pass through. Those waves carry heat away from your body to keep you cool.

*Part 2*

The future of fashion is not just about improving garments' existing functions. Some researchers have dreamt up wholly new uses for clothing — like turning wearers into walking power

Notes

- veg out のんびり過ごす
- are dreaming up ～ ～を考え出している
- comfier comfy「心地よい」の比較級
- pop-out spikes on the sole 靴底から飛び出すスパイク
- keep their footing 踏ん張る
- terrain 地形
- metal-organic framework 金属有機構造体
- war-torn 戦争で荒廃した
- attire 衣装、服装
- layer up 何層も重ねる
- humming through ～ ～を通じてぶんぶん音を立てる
- on the flip side その一方で
- pore 孔(あな)
- infrared wave 赤外線波
- garment 衣類、衣服
- power outlet 電源コンセント

outlets. Flexible solar panels sewn into fabric could soak up the sun to recharge phones or other devices on the go. And some types of fabric could harvest energy directly from a wearer's motion. Triboelectric materials, for example, can generate electricity when bent or flexed. (Friction between different parts of the material builds up charge, like rubbing your hair against a balloon.) Piezoelectric materials, which produce a charge when squeezed or twisted, could be fashioned into outfits, too.

While some fabrics help charge devices, others could serve as devices themselves. In one recent experiment, researchers stitched conductive thread into a t-shirt. This turned the shirt into an antenna that could send signals to a smartphone. Another team threaded fabric with magnetized copper and silver to write data into fabrics. Such data-packed fabric could be used as a hands-free key or form of ID.

Many of these ideas have not yet left the lab — and they're still pretty far from hitting retail racks. But inventors hope these and other innovations could someday let you get more from your wardrobe.

(475 words)

sewn into ～ ～に縫い込まれた
soak up the sun 太陽光線を吸収する
on the go（固定電源コンセントのない）外出先で
triboelectric 摩擦電気の
when bent or flexed たわめたり曲げたりするとき
piezoelectric 圧電性の
be fashioned into ～ ～に形作られる
conductive 導電性のある
magnetized 磁化された
far from hitting ～ ～に到達するにはほど遠い
retail racks（小売店等の）棚

# Exercises

KEY PHRASES

(　　)に適切な語句を語群から選び英文を完成させましょう。ただし、必要に応じて語形は変えること。

1. I tried to refresh myself by (　　　　　　　　　　) at the gym after doing the housework.
2. Some types of herbal tea will help the body (　　　　　　　　　　) fat.
3. Using a credit card (　　　　　　　　　　) an IC chip requires special caution.
4. After several minutes of anxiety, our airplane (　　　　　　　　　　) an air pocket.
5. A tiny packet of drugs was skillfully (　　　　　　　　　　) the lining of her coat.

| break down | embed with | pass through | sew into | work out |
|---|---|---|---|---|

IN-DEPTH REVIEW

本文の内容に合うようにa～cから(　　)に適切な語句を選びましょう。

t 1

1. (　　　　) is used to produce a wearable layer of protection from harmful chemicals.
   a. A metal-organic framework
   b. A lightweight shield
   c. One new spike shoe
2. Nanowires in the new fabric are expected to (　　　　).
   a. block the visible light by generating electricity
   b. keep the wearers warm by using their body heat
   c. reflect infrared waves by embedding them in the material

t 2

1. Triboelectric materials and piezoelectric materials help the researchers (　　　　).
   a. create a new type of solar panel
   b. develop self-powered outfits
   c. move their bodies smoothly
2. It is expected that (　　　　) in future.
   a. conductive thread stitched into a t-shirt will soak up the sun
   b. data-packed fabric could be replaced by a hands-free key
   c. the newly developed fabrics with various functions will go on the market

DL 09 CD1-30

## Summary

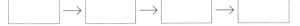

**以下の a ～ d を本文に出てきた順番に合うように並べ替え、それぞれの Part の要約文を作りましょう。最後に音声を聞いて確認しましょう。**

Part 1

☐ → ☐ → ☐ → ☐

a. Nanowires that are sewn into fabric could be used to keep you warm.

b. Our clothes could do far more than just make us relax or make a good impression.

c. Instead of providing us warmth, a new kind of fabric allows body heat to escape through tiny pores.

d. A new fabric coating may possibly protect people from harmful chemical compounds.

Part 2

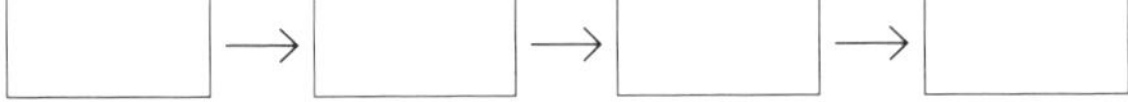

a. It will take some time before these new fabric devices are marketed on a large scale.

b. If personal data were to be packed into fabrics, you could wear, say, a t-shirt with your ID built into it.

c. Researchers are thinking of installing solar panels in fabric for the purpose of generating power.

d. Some types of clothes may be able to produce energy by using the wearer's motion.

## Writing Strategy

**日本語の意味に合うように [　　] 内の語 (句) を並べ替え、英文を完成させましょう。**

1. 東京に本拠を置く会社が、飛び出すスパイクを埋め込んだ靴底を開発した。
A [ *company* / *developed* / *pop-out* / *shoe soles* / *spikes* / *Tokyo-based* / *with* ] embedded in them.

_______________________________________________

2. もしも、柔軟性のあるソーラーパネルを布地に織り込むならば、発電ができるだろう。
Flexible solar panels [ *could* / *electricity* / *fabric* / *generate* / *if* / *into* / *sewn* ].

_______________________________________________

## Clue to Usage

### ハイフンでつなぐ複合形容詞

pop-out (ℓ. 9)やmetal-organic (ℓ. 13)、see-through (ℓ. 25)、hands-free (ℓ. 46)など、いろいろな品詞を自在にハイフンでつないで、一個の形容詞（複合形容詞）を作る。過去分詞を含む例も多く、war-torn countries「戦争で荒廃した国」(ℓ. 15) や data-packed fabric「データを詰め込んだ布地」(ℓ. 45)などのように使う。countries (that are) torn by warや fabric (that is) packed with dataといった表現よりはずっと身軽。

ex) a small-sized box / a full-grown giraffe

### 接続詞＋過去分詞

Part 2には when bent or flexed (ℓ. 35) や when squeezed or twisted (ℓ. 38) という見慣れない文型がある。どちらも、when they (=materials) are bentなどと丁寧に言うべきところをthey areの部分を省略した形。分詞構文（ふつうは接続詞並びに重複する主語などは省く）の意味合いを明瞭にするためにあえて接続詞を残したと考えてもよい。

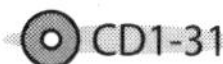


## Approaching the Contents

**質問文の下線部分を書き取り、解答をa～dから選びましょう。**

1 **Q:** In what way could our clothes ______________________________?

a. New clothes that have lots of tiny pores could protect you from infrared waves.
b. Equipped with pop-out spikes on the clothes, they could neutralize some chemicals.
c. Covered with special coatings, they could protect people from harmful substances.
d. If enough nanowires were built in, the clothes would carry heat away from your body.

2 **Q:** In what way can some kinds of ______________________________?

a. By recharging your devices including an iPhone.
b. By bending or squeezing the material, for instance.
c. By connecting the clothes' surface to a fixed power outlet.
d. By packing enough data in the fabric.

# Over to you!

以下の表では wearable technology の歴史を短く紹介しています。1 ～ 7 に適切な語を語群から選び、表中の英文を完成させましょう。ただし、必要に応じて語形は変えること。

| | |
|---|---|
| 1980s   | The Walkman became the most popular wearable music device throughout the 80s after being released by Sony Corporation in 1979. By releasing the first commercial full digital hearing aids in 1987, the (1. ) industry was also underwent a transformation during this decade. The device contained a body-worn processor with a hardwire connection and an ear-mounted transducer. |
| 1990s  | Steve Mann, a Canadian engineer, inventor, and researcher, invented the wearable wireless webcam in 1994. This oversized webcam has made the use of future IoT technologies easier. He is sometimes called the "Father of Wearable Computing." Smart clothing (2. ) and wearable technology conferences also rapidly gained popularity. |
| 2000s 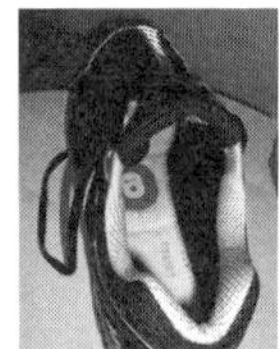 | This decade was a memorable one for the history of wearable technology. We saw an (3. ) in fantastic wearable technology with the introduction of Bluetooth headsets, Fitbits, and the Nike plus iPod Sport Kit. In the case of Bluetooth, for example, people gave an open-armed (4. ) to the device, which allows computers, mobile phones, and other devices to communicate with each other without being (5. ) by wires. |
| 2010s  | The first half of the period was the turning point for wearable technology. Google Glass entered the scene in 2013, while the Apple Watch debuted in 2015 and was (6. ) by The Oculus Rift Headset in 2016. Then the gaming industry is continuing to add newer AR (Augmented Reality) and VR (Virtual Reality) headsets, while clothing designers have been (7. ) smart clothing to the mainstream. |

| bring | connect | exhibition | explosion | follow | healthcare | welcome |
|---|---|---|---|---|---|---|

# Unit 4

# Earth's Underground Water

## 見えない地下水に目を向ける

地下水は目に見えないところを流れているため、抱えている問題の多くが見えませんでした。こうした状況を大きく改善したのが科学の力です。人工衛星を利用した調査は広範囲に及ぶ地下の観測を可能にし、地球規模での地下水の分布や水分含有率などを明らかにしました。科学の力で可視化された諸問題は、悲鳴を上げている「水の惑星」の姿を映し出します。

## *Word Choice*

**日本語の意味に合うように a ～ f から適切な語を選びましょう。ただし、選択肢には解答と関係のないものもあります。**

t 1

| | |
|---|---|
| 1. 写真の下の短い説明文を読む | read the caption (　　　　) the photos |
| 2. 茂みの背後に潜む | (　　　　) behind the bushes |
| 3. 空気から水分を取り出す | (　　　　) moisture from the air |
| 4. 適切な衛生設備を利用できる | have access to proper (　　　　) |
| 5. 病気に強い作物を育てる | grow disease-resistant (　　　　) |

a. beneath　b. crops　c. extract　d. lurk　e. sanitation　f. wetlands

t 2

| | |
|---|---|
| 1. 激しい喉の渇きに苦しむ | suffer from a burning (　　　　) |
| 2. 戦争終結に向けた外交努力を強化する | (　　　　) diplomatic efforts to stop the war |
| 3. 人類の生存を脅かす | (　　　　) the survival of human beings |
| 4. 壊れた下水管を修理する | repair the broken (　　　　) pipes |
| 5. 水の浄化に塩素を使う | use chlorine to (　　　　) water |

a. inject　b. intensify　c. purify　d. sewage　e. thirst　f. threaten

DL 11 CD1-32 ~ CD1-39

## Reading

### *Let's learn about Earth's secret stash of underground water*

Part 1

Walking over water might sound like a miracle. In fact, people do it all the time. How? Almost all of the world's liquid freshwater lies underground. This stash beneath our feet is called groundwater.

Earth is a water planet, but most of its $H_2O$ is in the oceans. Only about 2.5 percent of the planet's water is freshwater. Of that, nearly 69 percent is frozen in glaciers and ice caps. About 30 percent is groundwater — much more than the meager 1.2 percent that flows through rivers and fills lakes.

Groundwater is found almost everywhere on Earth. It lurks under mountains, plains and even deserts. Tiny gaps between rocks and soil grains soak up and hold this water like a sponge, forming buried bodies of water called aquifers. Together, they hold about 60 times as much water as the world's lakes and rivers combined.

Groundwater is a key part of Earth's water cycle. Rain and melted snow seep down into the ground. There, the water can stay for thousands of years. Some groundwater naturally leaks out onto Earth's surface through springs. It also feeds into lakes, rivers, and wetlands. People extract groundwater through wells for drinking, sanitation, watering crops, and other uses. In fact, people extract more than 200 times as much groundwater from Earth as oil every year.

Part 2

Most groundwater is used to water crops. But this water also quenches the thirst of some 2 billion people worldwide, including half the population of the United States.

As human-caused climate change dries out parts of the planet, demand for groundwater may rise. At the same time, climate change may intensify storms. Heavier rains are more likely to rush straight into streams and storm drains than soak

Notes

stash 隠されているもの

ice cap 氷冠

soak up ～ ～を吸い上げる

aquifer 帯水層

seep down into ～ ～にしみこむ

wetland 湿地

quenches 渇きをいやす

storm drain 雨水管

into the soil. So, there may be less groundwater to go around.

Many of the world's aquifers already seem to be drying up. Twenty-one of Earth's 37 biggest aquifers are shrinking, satellite data show. The most dried-out aquifers are near big cities, farms, or arid regions. As groundwater stores dwindle, they hold less water to refill rivers and streams, threatening freshwater ecosystems. In California, sucking the ground dry may even be triggering small earthquakes.

Meanwhile, human activity pollutes groundwater in many places. Arsenic from farming or mining seeps into aquifers. So do chemicals that are injected underground to flush out oil or gas in a process called fracking. Electronic waste from discarded devices and sewage have also tainted groundwater. What can be done? Cutting back on pollution and finding new ways to purify groundwater may help protect this precious resource.

(425 words)

arid 乾燥した
dwindle 減少する

sucking the ground dry 地面(から水分)を吸い上げつくす
trigger ～を引き起こす

meanwhile 一方で
pollutes ～を汚染する
arsenic ヒ素
mining 採掘
are injected 注入された

discarded device 破棄された機器類
have also tainted ～ (主語)もまた～を汚した

*Further Notes*

ℓ.42 **fracking** 水圧破砕法。石油や天然ガスの採掘方法のひとつで hydraulic fracking とも言われる。地下の岩石層に砂や化学物質を混ぜた大量の水(フラッキング水)を注入し、亀裂を生じさせてガスや石油を採取する。化学物質による地下水脈や土壌の汚染、周辺地域の水不足、ずさんな廃液処理、地震発生の引き金になる可能性などの問題点が指摘され、近年、この方法を禁止する動きが顕著になっている。

## Exercises

KEY PHRASES

(　　)に適切な語句を語群から選び英文を完成させましょう。ただし、必要に応じて語形は変えること。

1. The sponge will (　　　　　　　　) the spilled water almost immediately.
2. News of the company's financial troubles began to (　　　　　　　　).
3. All the data in each security camera should (　　　　　　　　) the hard drive in the guards' office.
4. Our uniforms will soon (　　　　　　　　) under the strong sun.
5. Due to the high increase in prices, we need to (　　　　　　　　) our household spending.

| cut back on | dry out | feed into | leak out | soak up |
|---|---|---|---|---|

IN-DEPTH REVIEW

本文の内容に合うようにa～cから(　　)に適切な語句を選びましょう。

Part 1

1. Groundwater (　　　　).
   a. does not contain any freshwater
   b. is hidden from view
   c. is not found in desert areas
2. People can use groundwater to (　　　　).
   a. extract oil
   b. produce our food
   c. build wells

Part 2

1. Data from satellites reveal that (　　　　).
   a. the number of aquifers is decreasing
   b. more than half of the aquifers in the U.S. are in danger
   c. some aquifers are getting smaller
2. The decrease in the amount of groundwater (　　　　).
   a. damages freshwater ecosystems
   b. contaminates the aquifer
   c. triggers big earthquakes around the world

DL 12 CD1-40

## Summary

**以下の a ～ d を本文に出てきた順番に合うように並べ替え、それぞれの Part の要約文を作りましょう。最後に音声を聞いて確認しましょう。**

1 [ ] → [ ] → [ ] → [ ]

a. Groundwater is extracted for various purposes such as watering crops.

b. It may sound strange, but groundwater exists even under deserts.

c. Little of the Earth's water flows through rivers.

d. Seeping down into the ground, water can stay there for thousands of years.

2 [ ] → [ ] → [ ] → [ ]

a. Even a small earthquake can be triggered by sucking the ground dry.

b. Along with watering crops, groundwater is used to satisfy the thirst of many people.

c. Various types of chemicals are polluting this precious resource — groundwater.

d. Groundwater may become less than needed. In fact, big aquifers are shrinking.

## Writing Strategy

**日本語の意味に合うように [　　] 内の語 (句) を並べ替え、英文を完成させましょう。**

1. 帯水層が小さくなって、川や湖に十分な水を供給しないならば、水の生態系は脅かされるだろう。
Freshwater ecosystems could be threatened [ *aquifers* / *don't* / *dwindling* / *enough water* / *feed* / *if* / *into* ] the rivers and lakes.

_______________________________________________

2. 地球の帯水層にはたくさんの水がある。実際、そこには、湖と川を合わせたよりもおよそ 60 倍多くの水がある。
Earth's aquifers contain lots of freshwater. In fact, [ *approximately* / *hold* / *more* / *60* / *than* / *they* / *times* / *water* ] the rivers and lakes combined.

_______________________________________________

## Clue to Usage

### in factの「実際(は)」

Part 1 には、In fact, people do it all the time. (ℓ. 1) と In fact, people extract ... every year. (ℓ. 21) のように in fact を含む文が 2 つある。in fact には ①今述べたことを「実際に (本当に) そうなのだ」と強める意味合いと、②「実際は (本当は) そうではなく」、と新たな説明を導入する場合の 2 通りの用法がある。易しい例文を考えてみる。His painting is amazing. Yes, he is a genius, in fact. とくれば①の例で、「本当に天才だ」の意味。He says he is still young, but in fact, he is 80 years old. は②の例で「本当は若くない」を意味する。上記の本文の例は、前者が②、後者が①の使い方である。

### 倍数の表し方

数量の比較で「～の…倍」というときは、60 times as much water as ... (ℓ. 14) や 200 times as much groundwater from Earth as ... (ℓ. 22) のように表現する。同等比較のas ～ as に「…倍」を示す ... times をつける。

ex) The new bridge is three times as long as the old one.

倍の長さなら twice as long as ～, 半分なら half as long as ～ と表現する。なお、比較級を使って、The new bridge is three times longer than the old one. と書くこともできるし、形容詞を名詞に代えて、The new bridge is three times the length of the old one. といった表現もある。サイズの比較なら twice the size of ～、重さならhalf the weight of ～ などのように表現する。

DL 13 CD1-41

## Approaching the Contents

**質問文の下線部分を書き取り、解答を a ～ d から選びましょう。**

Part 1

Q: Where on Earth do you think ________________________________?

a. Nearly 70 percent of Earth's $H_2O$ is frozen.
b. As for liquid freshwater, almost all of it exists underground.
c. Most of the Earth's water is in the ocean. And freshwater is only 1.2 percent of all.
d. Water from glaciers, for example, seeps into the ground, which waters crops.

Part 2

Q: According to the passage, ________________________________ today?

a. An urgent issue is that many aquifers have been shrinking.
b. Due to severe storms, Earth's layers are supplied with too much water.
c. Sea water is being polluted as a result of recent climate change.
d. As satellite data show, aquifers under the deserts have been hit hard by climate change.

# Over to you!

1～3 は underground water について書かれた文章です。[　　] に入る適切な語を Keywords から選びましょう。また、提示されている英文が正しい場合は T、誤っている場合は F で答えましょう。

**Keywords** collected / filled / responsible / separated

1. You have very little chance to see groundwater with your own eyes, but, actually, it exists in great amounts under your feet. When falling to the ground, water from rain and snow flows down rivers or collects in lakes and wetlands, or just melts and evaporates quickly, but some soaks deep into the ground and stay there. Below the surface soil, the ground is composed of rock and soil grains and can be abundantly [　　　　] with such slow-moving hidden water, which forms huge storehouses called aquifers.

   [T / F] Only a small quantity of groundwater exists below the surface soil.

   [T / F] Some rainwater flows down rivers soon, but some soaks into the ground.

2. Water scarcity is not uncommon in developing countries. Climate change and war conflicts are [　　　　] for it. Also, aging waterworks and poor maintenance are to blame. Tens of millions of people are afflicted by poor water quality and water shortages which can adversely affect people's lives. In fact, many children die from water-related illnesses every year. As you might imagine, groundwater may solve the problem. For example, Hope Rising Together, an NPO working in Africa, has been building wells to provide poverty-stricken communities with sufficient clean water.

   [T / F] Many people become ill by drinking water that is not good for their health.

   [T / F] Digging wells could be one of the efficient ways to solve the water shortage problem.

3. Nobody can deny the importance of groundwater resources. Not only used as drinking and sanitary water but a large amount of groundwater is pumped up for farming in arid regions of the world. The problem is, more water than is [　　　　] by rain and snow may be used for watering crops. The inevitable result is that the aquifers are in danger of running short of their stored water, even if they are large enough at the moment.

   [T / F] Farmers could pump up as much water as they like for growing crops in dry seasons.

   [T / F] Huge aquifers could supply enough water to great stretches of farmland throughout the year.

# Unit 5

# Pareidolia — Imaginary Faces

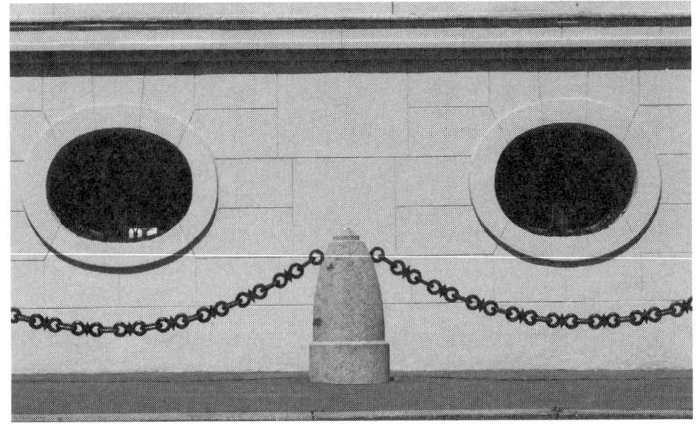

**「パレイドリア」から見える偏見**

雲や樹皮、石の表面を見ているうちに、人の顔が浮かんでくるような気がした経験はありませんか。ある科学者が、顔が浮かんできそうな物を被験者に見てもらい、浮かんできた顔の性別を被験者に尋ねたところ、回答に偏りが見られました。今度、顔が浮かんでくる経験をした時にその顔の性別を自問してみて下さい。

## Word Choice

**日本語の意味に合うように a ～ f から適切な語を選びましょう。ただし、選択肢には解答と関係のないものもあります。**

Part 1

| | | |
|---|---|---|
| 1. | 想像上の動物についてネットで調べる | do a web search for (　　　　) animals |
| 2. | 彼の無実の確かな証拠を発見する | (　　　　) positive proof of his innocence |
| 3. | 鋭い知覚を自慢する | boast of a keen sense of (　　　　) |
| 4. | ボランティアを募ることを提案する | propose to (　　　　) some volunteers |
| 5. | その事柄を異なる角度から見る | (　　　　) the issue from a different angle |

a. imaginary　b. perception　c. recruit　d. uncover　e. view　f. wonder

Part 2

| | | |
|---|---|---|
| 1. | 少数派に対する偏見を排除する | eliminate (　　　　) against minorities |
| 2. | その宝石を本物と判断する | (　　　　) the jewel as genuine |
| 3. | 製品のその他の情報を求める | ask for (　　　　) information about a product |
| 4. | 長いまつげをしている | have long (　　　　) |
| 5. | 何気ない言葉に意味を持たせる | (　　　　) meaning to a casual remark |

a. assign　b. bias　c. extra　d. gender　e. judge　f. lashes

## Reading

### Americans tend to see imaginary faces as male, not female

*Part 1*

Notes

Have you ever seen the outline of a face in a cloud? Or perhaps in the pattern of your carpet? Or some other everyday object? This phenomenon is very common. It's called pareidolia. Much is still unknown about how people perceive such imaginary, or "illusory" faces. But a new study has uncovered one curious detail. People are more likely to see illusory faces as male than female. Researchers shared that finding on February 1. It appeared in the *Proceedings of the National Academy of Sciences*.

illusory 架空の、錯覚を起こさせる

The research was led by Susan Wardle. She works at the National Institutes of Health in Bethesda, Md. This cognitive neuroscientist is fascinated by illusory faces. "They're an example of face perception that's incorrect," she says. "And often by studying the mistakes of our brain, we can better understand how it works."

Bethesda, Md. メリーランド州ベセスダ
cognitive neuroscientists 認知神経科学者

One day while looking at photos of illusory faces in the lab, Wardle wondered: "Where're all the female faces?" Even though the faces appeared in nonliving objects with no gender, most appeared male to her.

Wardle was curious whether other people shared this bias. So she and her colleagues recruited over 3,800 people online. All were adults living in the United States. These volunteers viewed about 250 photos of illusory faces. The faces appeared in a variety of objects, from potatoes to suitcases. Participants labeled each one as male, female, or neither.

bias 偏見

label ～を分類する

*Part 2*

Illusory faces were labeled male about four times as often as they were female. Both male and female participants showed that bias. About 80 percent of people labeled more images male than female. Only 3 percent judged more images to be female than male.

"There's this asymmetry in our perception," Wardle says. An illusory face is a very basic pattern of a face. Given such a basic pattern, "we're more likely to see it as male," Wardle says. "It requires additional features to see it as female." This makes sense, she adds. Think of female emojis and Lego characters. They are often distinguished from male ones by extra features, such as bigger lips and longer lashes.

asymmetry 非対称、不釣り合い
Given ~, ~を与えられると、

It's not yet clear why people assume simple faces are male, Wardle says. But in a more recent study, her team found the same gender bias in kids as young as five. This suggests the bias arises early in life.

"I was not surprised that people would assign gender to illusory faces," says Sheng He. But he was surprised by the strength of the gender bias that Wardle's team discovered. He is a cognitive neuroscientist too. He works at the Chinese Academy of Sciences in Beijing. Future studies, he says, could test whether the same bias exists among people in other cultures.

(447 words)

*Further Notes*

*ℓ*.4 **pareidolia** パレイドリア。ある対象から受ける視覚や聴覚の刺激によって、その対象が実際とは異なるもの（多くの場合は馴染みの深いもの）として認知、解釈される心理現象。例としては、壁のしみや机の木目、雲などを見て、人間の顔が見えてくる現象が挙げられる。

*ℓ*.8 ***Proceedings of the National Academy of Sciences*** 『米国科学アカデミー紀要』米国科学アカデミーが発行する機関誌。1915 年創刊。自然科学全領域に加え、社会科学、人文科学も対象としている。総合科学雑誌として、『ネイチャー』誌、『サイエンス』誌に並ぶ高い評価を得ている。

*ℓ*.11 **National Institutes of Health** アメリカ国立衛生研究所。1887 年に設立されたアメリカでもっとも歴史のある医学研究の拠点機関。専門分野を扱う研究所のほか、付属施設、図書館、事務局などから構成されている。

*ℓ*.35 **Lego** 通称「レゴブロック」として知られる、プラスチック製の組み立てブロック玩具。レゴ（LEGO）は、デンマークの玩具会社の名前だが、同社が製造する玩具を指す時にも使われる。

*ℓ*.45 **Chinese Academy of Sciences** 中国科学院。1949 年に設立された中国における自然科学とハイテク総合科学の最高機関。世界的に最高レベルの評価を得ている。

## Exercises

**KEY PHRASES** **(　　)に適切な語句を語群から選び英文を完成させましょう。ただし、必要に応じて語形は変えること。**

1. We need to prepare for the worst events that (　　　　　　　　　　) happen.
2. The expedition team last year (　　　　　　　　　　) a world-famous explorer.
3. Many listeners will (　　　　　　　　　　) the musical voice of the new radio DJ.
4. The twins can (　　　　　　　　　　) each other by their hairstyles.
5. When young, the scientist (　　　　　　　　　　) an odd fellow because of his strange behavior.

| be distinguished from | be fascinated by | be led by | be likely to | be labeled as |
|---|---|---|---|---|

**IN-DEPTH REVIEW** **本文の内容に合うようにa～cから(　　)に適切な語句を選びましょう。**

t 1

1. Susan Wardle thinks that (　　　　) the errors made by brains.
   a. cognitive neuroscientists can explain the mechanism of
   b. we can learn more about the brain functions from the study of
   c. pareidolia is hard to understand because of
2. Wardle's experiment needed (　　　　).
   a. 250 people living in the United States
   b. more than 200 photos showing illusory faces
   c. nonhuman objects appearing male to her

t 2

1. A Lego character with long lashes (　　　　) because of the extra feature.
   a. is often regarded as a female
   b. will cause asymmetry in our perception
   c. looks like a living female
2. What surprised Sheng He was (　　　　).
   a. people's behavior that assigned gender to illusory faces
   b. the power of gender bias among people
   c. the potential of cognitive neuroscience

DL 15 CD1-50

## Summary

**以下の a ～ d を本文に出てきた順番に合うように並べ替え、それぞれの Part の要約文を作りましょう。最後に音声を聞いて確認しましょう。**

Part 1

□ → □ → □ → □

a. A neuroscientist was extremely interested in illusory faces, as they are related to the issue of incorrect perception.

b. It occurred to her that most of the illusory faces appeared male rather than female.

c. We have not yet discovered precisely how we come to perceive imaginary faces.

d. The researchers had people view many photos of illusory faces to decide whether the gender bias really exists.

Part 2

□ → □ → □ → □

a. The same gender bias as adults showed was found in kids as young as five.

b. It is not yet clear whether such gender bias exists in other cultures.

c. As many as 80 percent of the volunteers assumed illusory-face photos were male.

d. If people are given simple faces, they are likely to see them as male, not female.

## Writing Strategy

**日本語の意味に合うように [　　] 内の語を並べ替え、英文を完成させましょう。**

1. 新たな証拠が発見されたことを考えると、警察はその会計士を逮捕することになるだろう。

[ *been* /*evidence* / *found* / *given* / *has* / *new* / *that* ], the police will arrest the accountant.

______________________________

2. この事業を立ち上げるのに十分な資金を集められるかどうか、と私は思っていたのです。

I [ *could* / *collect* / *enough* / *was* / *we* / *whether* / *wondering* ] money to start the project.

______________________________

## Clue to Usage

### 「～かどうか」のwhether

本文中にはWardle was curious whether ～ (ℓ. 20) と、Further studies ... could test whether ～ (ℓ. 46) のように、whether を使った文が２つある。どちらも名詞節を導く接続詞で「～かどうか(ということ)」と意味をとることができ、ifとほぼ同じ用法である。ただ、whetherには「～であろうとなかろうと」という意味の副詞節を導く接続詞としての使い方もあるため、区別が必要だ。以下は副詞節の例文である。

ex) You will be late whether you go by bus or train. / I can trust her whether her story is true or not.

### Givenのトリセツ

文頭にくる過去分詞形のGiven ～, は扱いづらいため、以下に分類して説明する。

① (過去分詞そのものとして使う)分詞構文の場合、例えば Given the chance, I could do it by myself. という文を、接続詞を使って書き換えると、If I were given the chance, I could do ... となる。本文に出てくるGiven such a basic pattern (ℓ. 32)という表現もこの型と同じである。

② 前置詞のように使う場合、以下の２つの文は同じ意味に取ることができる。
Given the bad weather, I think they worked rather well.
Considering the bad weather, I think they worked rather well.

③ 接続詞のように使う場合、Givenの後ろにthat節がくるため接続詞の扱いになる。
Given that the weather was terrible, the result was better than expected.

DL 16 CD1-51

## Approaching the Contents

**質問文の下線部分を書き取り、解答をａ～ｄから選びましょう。**

1 **Q:** Why did the researchers recruit volunteers and ______________________ ?

**a.** The aim was to gather adults who lived in the U.S. and could join the test.
**b.** They examined whether people would show some bias toward illusory faces.
**c.** Because many people were fascinated by various phenomena of illusion.
**d.** Because they need to cure injured brains.

2 **Q:** Why did so many participants judge ______________________ ?

**a.** Because volunteers were often given lots of samples of male faces.
**b.** Because the gender bias was deeply rooted in the minds of young adults.
**c.** Because such illusory faces tend to lack features that suggest they are female.
**d.** Because they knew such a bias did not exist among young people.

# Over to you!

**1～3 は Pareidolia について書かれた文章です。[　　] に入る適切な語を Keywords から選びましょう。また、提示されている英文が正しい場合は T、誤っている場合は F で答えましょう。**

**Keywords** appropriate / eternal / psychological / stereotypical

**1.** It happens that we sometimes detect or imagine some meaningful figures (though they are not real) in the objects we see. This tendency of perception is called pareidolia. You can find curious images of animals, human faces, etc., in landscapes such as clouds in the sky or mountain rock formations. Common images of kitchen utensils, vegetables like potatoes or tomatoes, or even a block of cheese could often be interpreted as human faces. Whether funny or scary depending on the viewer's impression, such illusory images may be a unique expression of our [　　　　] responses to the outer world.

[ T / F ] Various natural objects could be interpreted as meaningful figures even if they are mere illusions.

[ T / F ] Although you can see human faces in rock formations, you rarely see them in other common objects.

**2.** In the past, people extended their imagined perceptions beyond the Earth and identified various constellations among the stars, like Orion and Scorpius. Today, it is reported that the Hubble Space Telescope has located a smiley face formed by two galaxies. Closer to home, the Moon rabbit is also a familiar pareidolia. In Japanese and Korean folklore, the rabbit is interpreted as pounding rice in a mortar to make *mochi*. In China, people imagined that a rabbit is pounding herbs to make a magical remedy for [　　　　] life.

[ T / F ] Orion and Scorpius form a smiling face—a new pareidolia created by a precision telescope.

[ T / F ] In China, the rabbit is seen as pounding rice in a mortar to make *mochi*.

**3.** Why are illusory faces looked on as male rather than female? To be judged as feminine faces, they must have so-called womanlike features, such as bright eyes, plump cheeks, long eyelashes, etc. In one word, they need well-proportioned features to be identified as women. Of course, these are [　　　　] ideas of a desirable woman. People have established such gender-biased ideas over a long period of time. No wonder such images should be quite different from 'basic' patterns perceived on plain inanimate objects that are often lacking in womanly grace.

[ T / F ] If an illusionary face has well-proportioned features, it may possibly be interpreted as a woman's face.

[ T / F ] Gender-biased assumptions have been strictly rejected in the world of pareidolia.

# Unit 6 Robotic Finger

## 人間との距離を縮めるロボット

日本の大学の研究室で指型ロボットが誕生しました。思わずひいてしまうほど人間らしく見える理由は、生きた皮膚を利用した点にあります。今はまだ指1本だけですが、従来の労働力の代わりとして人間らしいロボットが求められる介護の現場をはじめ、各方面から開発に大きな期待が寄せられています。

## Word Choice

**日本語の意味に合うように a 〜 f から適切な語を選びましょう。ただし、選択肢には解答と関係のないものもあります。**

t1

1. 新政府への円滑な移行を達成する　achieve a (　　　　) transition to the new government
2. タンパク質をエネルギーに変える　convert (　　　　) into energy
3. 聞き覚えのない声にぞっとする　get a (　　　　) feeling from the strange voice
4. 顕微鏡で生体組織を観察する　examine the body (　　　　) under a microscope
5. 幹細胞研究にエネルギーを注ぐ　(　　　　) energy into stem-cell research

| a. creepy | b. layer | c. pour | d. protein | e. seamless | f. tissue |
|---|---|---|---|---|---|

t2

1. 新しいワクチンへの道を拓く　(　　　　) the way for a new vaccine
2. 伸縮性のあるマスクを大量生産する　produce (　　　　) masks on a large scale
3. 異分野の技術を融合する　(　　　　) some technologies from different fields
4. 彼の魅力的な性格に心を奪われる　fall in love with his (　　　　) character
5. 赤ちゃんの足をぬるま湯につける　(　　　　) the baby's feet in lukewarm water

| a. appealing | b. bathe | c. merge | d. nutrient | e. pave | f. stretch |
|---|---|---|---|---|---|

DL 17 CD1-52 ~ CD1-61

## Reading

### *This robotic finger is covered in living human skin*

*Part 1*

Notes

Robots that blend in with real people may be one step closer to reality.

A team of researchers has grown living human skin around a robotic finger. The goal is to someday build cyborgs to appear truly human. Those robots could have more seamless interactions with people, the researchers say. That might prove useful in the medical care and service industries. But whether machines disguised as people would be more likable — or just plain creepy — is probably a matter of opinion.

likable 好感が持てる

creepy 気味の悪い

Biohybrid engineer Shoji Takeuchi led the research. He and his colleagues at the University of Tokyo in Japan shared their new development on June 9 in *Matter*.

Covering a robotic finger in living skin took a few steps. First, the researchers covered the finger in a blend of collagen and fibroblasts. Collagen is a protein found in human tissue. Fibroblasts are cells found in human skin. The mix of collagen and fibroblasts settled into a base layer of skin around the finger. That layer is called the dermis.

collagen コラーゲン

fibroblast 線維芽細胞

dermis 真皮

The team then poured a liquid onto the finger. This liquid contained human cells known as keratinocytes (Kair-ah-TIN-oh-sites). Those cells formed an outer layer of skin, or epidermis. After two weeks, the skin covering the robotic finger was a few millimeters (0.1 inches) thick. That's about as thick as real human skin.

keratinocyte 角化細胞

epidermis 表皮

*Part 2*

University of Tokyo researchers covered this robotic finger in living human skin. Their achievement paves the way for ultrarealistic cyborgs.

paves the way for ~ ~への道を拓く

This lab-made skin was strong and stretchy. It didn't break when the robot finger bent. It also could heal itself. The team tested this by making a small cut on the robotic finger. Then, they covered the wound with a collagen bandage. Fibroblast cells on the finger merged the bandage with the rest of the skin within a week.

bandage 包帯

"This is very interesting work and an important step forward in the field," says Ritu Raman. She's an engineer at the Massachusetts Institute of Technology in Cambridge. She was not involved in the research. But she, too, builds machines with living parts.

"Biological materials are appealing because they can ... sense and adapt to their environments," Raman says. In the future, she'd like to see living robot skin embedded with nerve cells to help robots sense their surroundings.

embedded with ～ ～が埋め込まれている

But a cyborg couldn't wear the current lab-grown skin out and about just yet. The robot finger spent most of its time soaking in a soup of nutrients that cells need to survive. So, a robot wearing this skin would have to bathe often in a nutrient broth. Or it would need some other complex skincare routine.

broth スープ

(435 words)

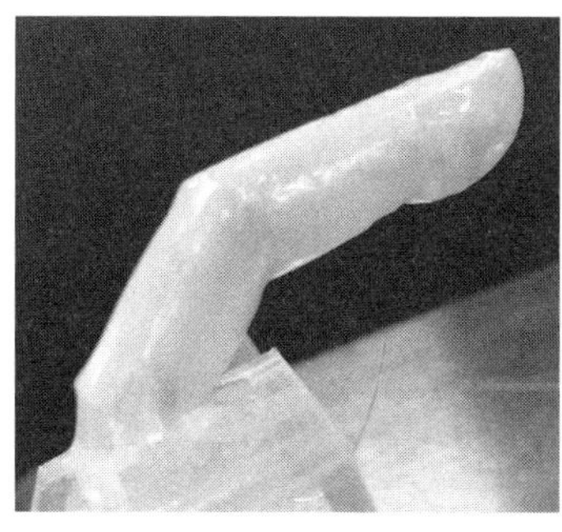

## *Further Notes*

ℓ.4 **cyborg** 竹内氏の研究室では cyborg（サイボーグ）ではなく、Biohybrid Robot と呼んでいる。cyborg は人間をベースに機械と融合していくものだが、この研究は機械をベースに生体素材を取り入れ生体機能を獲得していくものであるため、実際は cyborg ではなく android（アンドロイド）に近い。

ℓ.12 ***Matter*** 基礎から応用、ナノからマクロまで、材料科学全般を網羅する月刊学術雑誌。

ℓ.36 **Massachusetts Institute of Technology** マサチューセッツ工科大学（MIT）。世界のトップクラスに数えられるアメリカ合衆国の私立大学。設立は 1861 年。マサチューセッツ州ケンブリッジに本部を置く。複数の専攻分野の中で、特に工学と科学における研究は世界をリードする質の高さを誇る。

## Exercises

KEY PHRASES　(　　) に適切な語句を語群から選び英文を完成させましょう。ただし、必要に応じて語形は変えること。

1. The newcomers succeeded in (　　　　　　　　　　) the local people.
2. The thieves were (　　　　　　　　　　) security guards.
3. Having no experience, he had some difficulties in (　　　　　　　　　　) the dormitory.
4. She has been actively (　　　　　　　　　　) volunteer work in various nursing homes.
5. Considering her age, it's far beyond her power to (　　　　　　　　　　) such a harsh reality.

| adapt to | blend in with | disguise as | involve in | settle into |
|---|---|---|---|---|

IN-DEPTH REVIEW　本文の内容に合うようにa～cから(　　)に適切な語句を選びましょう。

Part 1

1. Researchers developed a robotic finger (　　　　).
   a. coated with real human skin offered by a researcher
   b. wearing the material discovered in the lab by chance
   c. wrapped in artificial skin that acts like living human skin
2. It took 14 days for the lab-made skin to (　　　　).
   a. cover up the whole robotic finger
   b. grow almost as thick as human skin
   c. make human cells form an epidermis

Part 2

1. The skin, which demonstrated the ability to (　　　　), is stretchy.
   a. become a super realistic cyborg
   b. heal itself
   c. produce a collagen bandage
2. The researchers must never forget to (　　　　) to keep it alive.
   a. leave the finger for some time in a special liquid
   b. apply skincare cream to the finger
   c. change the old skin to fresh skin

## Summary

**以下の a ～ d を本文に出てきた順番に合うように並べ替え、それぞれの Part の要約文を作りましょう。最後に音声を聞いて確認しましょう。**

1 [    ] → [    ] → [    ] → [    ]

a. Some people may be disgusted at the strange idea of a robotic finger.

b. Robots wearing human-like skin might be useful in the medical care field.

c. The liquid that contained human cells developed into the outer layer of skin.

d. In the beginning, collagen and fibroblasts were blended to make a base layer of skin.

2 [    ] → [    ] → [    ] → [    ]

a. One of the strengths of biological materials is they can adapt to their environments.

b. For the present, the robot finger has to be soaked frequently in a soup of nutrients.

c. Researchers hope to someday create a robot skin embedded with nerve cells.

d. Even if the robotic finger were injured, it manages to cure itself.

## Writing Strategy

**日本語の意味に合うように [　　] 内の語 (句) を並べ替え、英文を完成させましょう。**

1. 休息と十分な栄養をとりなさい。そうすれば、1週間のうちに出歩けるようになります。
   Take a rest and enough nutrition, and [ *and* / *about* / *be* / *out* / *will* / *within* / *you* ] a week.

   ______________________________

2. 私は、傷に包帯を巻くという応急手当さえ、いまはまだ受けていません。
   I haven't received even the first-aid treatment with [ *a bandage* / *covering* / *just* / *the wound* / *yet* ].

   ______________________________

## Clue to Usage

### out and aboutの読み取り

But a cyborg couldn't wear the current lab-grown skin out and about just yet. (ℓ. 43)で使われるout and aboutは「外へ出て動ける状態」にある、という意味。この表現はそもそも次の例文のように「病気が癒えて動けるようになる状態」を指す。

ex) She is making a speedy recovery from the operation. So she will be out and about soon.

「起き上がってくる」イメージも持つため、out and aboutではなく up and aboutでもよい。次のように病気の回復とは離れて使われることもある。

ex) Be careful about the traffic when you are out and about.

また米語ではabout ではなくaroundとする方が普通。around とaboutの共存はfool around (about)やhang around (about) といった動詞句にも表れる。

### not ... just yetのニュアンス

上記でも紹介した文の末尾の表現、just yet (ℓ. 44)にも注意してほしい。全体が否定文のため「まだ～でない」という意味に取れそうだが、not ... just yetのようにjustが入ると、「今はまだ／まだすぐには～でない」というニュアンスになる。否定だけして終わるのではなく「近いうちには実現しそうだ」という期待も持たせる。

以上２点のポイントをまとめるとℓ. 43の文は「しかし、実験室育ちの現段階の皮膚を、サイボーグが身にまとって動き回ることは、まだ、今すぐにはできないだろう」と訳すことができる。

DL 19 CD1-63

## Approaching the Contents

**質問文の下線部分を書き取り、解答を a ～ d から選びましょう。**

Part 1

Q: What was the first step toward ________________ a robotic finger?

a. Realizing the idea in the medical service industry.

b. Building cyborgs that are disguised as people.

c. Blending collagen and fibroblast together.

d. Publishing their findings in an academic journal.

Part 2

Q: Why isn't the current skin ________________________?

a. Ms. Raman is not involved in the research project.

b. Because the finger has to be soaked in a nutritious liquid for a long period.

c. It takes some time to collect lots of nerve cells.

d. Because it is not clear whether the cells can merge with the collagen.

# Over to you!

**以下はオーストラリアの Rachel からアメリカのカリフォルニア州の Tim へ送られたメールです。[　　] に適切な語を Keywords から選び、提示されているクイズにも答えましょう。**

**Keywords** abundant / elastic / slightest / vague

Dear Tim,

Have you read the 'robotic finger' article? When the author explains the steps used in covering the mechanical finger with 'a blend of collagen and fibroblast,' she sounds as if she were explaining a recipe for cooking: It was amusing.

Until recently, I've only had a very [　　　　] idea of collagen. My mom often talks about collagen supplements as she is always careful about maintaining her [　　　　] and glowing skin.

Now, my information is that collagen is the most [　　　　] protein in the body. The task of collagen is to bind various tissues in the body firmly together. Collagen plays a major role in strengthening bones, muscles, joints, and skin.

Collagen is produced naturally within the body. However, when you pass the peak of production around the age of 20 or so, the output of collagen starts to decline. So you are often advised to take in supplementary collagen by eating collagen-rich food, such as meat, fish, etc. Or, if you like, oral collagen supplements will also do, just as my mom prefers. You can choose from among many types: pills, powders, or liquids.

Let me give you a quick quiz: Are you ready? *What should be avoided if you are to maintain a healthy level of collagen in your body?*

Talk to you soon,
Rachel

Which is the correct answer?

**(1)** You should stay away from consuming excessive calories because they cause you to become obese and decrease the production of collagen.

**(2)** You should avoid staying in the sun for too long because UV rays will cause damage to the collagen in the skin layer.

**(3)** You should not take too many different supplements at one time because they are likely to cause harmful side effects in your digestive organs.

# Unit 7 Delicious Insect Food

## 昆虫食をおいしく食べる

食糧危機を避けるための食材として期待される昆虫食。栄養価の高さ、環境負荷の軽さ、生産コストの安さといった魅力を備えながらも食卓との距離はなかなか縮まりません。そこで科学者の登場です。においの分析でおいしそうな香りを発散させ、栄養はそのままに粉砕などで見かけをなくすレシピの開発が進みます。

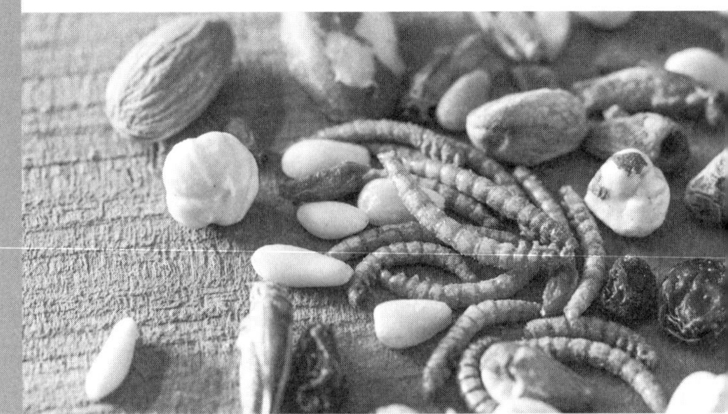

## Word Choice

**日本語の意味に合うように a ～ f から適切な語を選びましょう。ただし、選択肢には解答と関係のないものもあります。**

### Part 1

| | | |
|---|---|---|
| 1. | 台所からのおいしそうなにおいを楽しむ | enjoy the (　　　) smell from the kitchen |
| 2. | 靴箱から強烈なにおいを取り除く | eliminate the strong (　　　) from a shoe box |
| 3. | 家畜飼料を輸入する | import the feedstuff for (　　　) |
| 4. | 新進気鋭の人類学者と共同研究を始める | undertake a joint study with an up-and-coming (　　　) |
| 5. | 彼の話の信憑性を疑う | (　　　) the truth of his story |

a. anthropologist　b. appetizing　c. bug　d. livestock　e. odor　f. suspect

### Part 2

| | | |
|---|---|---|
| 1. | ノーベル賞受賞化学者と会う | meet a (　　　) who has won the Nobel Prize |
| 2. | アルミホイルで包んだ鶏を焼く | (　　　) the chicken in aluminum foil |
| 3. | その学術誌の質を評価する | (　　　) the quality of the academic journal |
| 4. | いじめへの嫌悪を示す | express (　　　) toward bullying |
| 5. | 彼女の不快なふるまいを我慢する | put up with her (　　　) manners |

a. chemist　b. disgusting　c. revulsion　d. rate　e. roast　f. yummy

## Reading

### New meat-scented food flavoring comes from sugar — and mealworms

Part 1

A spoonful of sugar may help the mealworms go down. That's what chemists in South Korea now report.

Adding sugars to powdered, cooked mealworms creates a new food seasoning to add to kitchen pantries. It has an appetizing "meat-like" odor, researchers reported on August 24. They shared their new findings at the American Chemical Society fall meeting in Chicago, Ill.

Some insects offer an environmentally friendly alternative to other sources of animal protein. For instance, they require less land and water to raise than typical livestock. Still, in the United States and other Western countries, most people have shown little interest in chomping down on bugs.

Indeed, notes Julie Lesnik, "There aren't a lot of people ready to fry up a whole skillet of crickets and eat them fresh." Lesnik, who did not take part in the new research, works at Wayne State University. It's in Detroit, Mich. Finding out how to make insect-based foods more appetizing could be key to getting them into more kitchens, says this biological anthropologist.

Just one successful product could have a snowball effect on other insect-based foods, says Brenden Campbell. He's an insect agriculturist based in Eugene, Ore., who has studied mealworms. He's even created a company called Planet Bugs. Its goal, in part, is to produce insect-based foods. "It's really great that this research is happening," he says of the new Korean study. "At any point," he suspects, people might take to the idea of insect-based foods. "And then it explodes."

Part 2

In Hee Cho is a chemist at Wonkwang University. It's in Iksan, South Korea. She works with mealworms. These are not true worms, but the larvae of darkling beetles (*Tenebrio*

Notes

mealworm ゴミムシダマシの昆虫(ℓ. 30 darkling beetle)の幼虫(ℓ. 30 larvae)のこと

seasoning 調味料、薬味
pantry 食品庫

American Chemical Society アメリカ化学会
Chicago, Ill. イリノイ州シカゴ
alternative to ～ ～に代わるもの

livestock 家畜

chomping down on ～ ～をむしゃむしゃ食べる

skillet 小鍋

Detroit, Mich. ミシガン州デトロイト

anthropologist 人類学者

Eugene, Ore. オレゴン州ユージーン

take to ～ ～が好きになる

*molitor*). A few years ago, Cho's team analyzed the odors given off as these larvae were steamed, roasted, or deep-fried. Steaming them produced a sweet smell, like corn. Roasting and frying them instead released chemicals into the air that were more like those given off by meat and seafood.

In its new work, her team keyed in on what recipe of mealworms, water, sugar, and cooking time produced particularly meaty scents. Then volunteers rated which of the smells seemed most yummy.

Using insects ground up or in seasonings, as Cho's team did, might help people get over their revulsion about eating insects whole, says Amy Wright. She, for one, has no problem with eating insects. A literature professor at Austin Peay State University in Clarksville, Tenn., Wright used to keep mealworms in her apartment. She'd add them to sandwiches and guacamole. In fact, she's such an insect-dining enthusiast that she's written a book on the topic.

"There are plenty of things that are disgusting to us," says Lesnik at Wayne State. But with engineering, people can get over it, she adds. "We're just seeing insects being treated like any other food. And yeah, we're talking aroma … but that's what the engineers of Doritos are doing."

(484 words)

deep-fried たっぷりの油で揚げられた

key in on ～ ～に注目する

yummy おいしい

guacamole グアカモーレ（アボガドディップ）

Doritos ドリトス（トルティーヤチップス）

*Further Notes*

ℓ.16 **Wayne State University** ウェイン州立大学。ミシガン州デトロイトにある大規模な州立大学。1868年創立。

ℓ.20 **snowball effect** 雪だるま効果。物事の重要性や大きさが加速しながら増すことを示す比喩表現。

ℓ.28 **Wonkwang University** 圓光（ウォングァン）大学校。大韓民国全羅北道益山市にある総合大学。

ℓ.43 **Austin Peay State University** オースティン・ピー州立大学。テネシー州クラークスビルにある州立の総合大学。

## Exercises

KEY PHRASES

**(　　)に適切な語句を語群から選び英文を完成させましょう。ただし、必要に応じて語形は変えること。**

1. I decided to (　　　　　　　　　　) a clinical study held in our lab.
2. Our manager (　　　　　　　　　　) our idea and allocated some funds for our project.
3. Inspector Morse (　　　　　　　　　　) the fingerprints that were left on the gun.
4. She asked me to (　　　　　　　　　　) some seeds until they turn into paste.
5. The company finally succeeded in (　　　　　　　　　　) the financial crisis.

| get over　　grind up　　key in on　　take part in　　take to |
|---|

IN-DEPTH REVIEW

**本文の内容に合うようにa～cから(　　)に適切な語句を選びましょう。**

t 1

1. (　　　　), bugs are not appealing to most people in the U.S.
   a. Because of the sweet taste coming from a spoonful of sugar
   b. In spite of their potential as a new source of protein
   c. In order to keep enough space for raising livestock
2. According to Brenden Campbell, (　　　　).
   a. people are sure to accept the idea of eating insects in no time
   b. his company Planet Bugs has already achieved its goal
   c. the new research carried out by Korean chemists will be worthwhile

t 2

1. In Hee Cho's team found out that (　　　　).
   a. the larvae released different smells according to how they were cooked
   b. a meaty smell was the most popular among volunteers
   c. the larvae gave off a sweet smell when fried
2. Amy Write thinks that (　　　　).
   a. her readers keep mealworms in their houses just like her
   b. people might eat insects if they couldn't actually see them in their food
   c. some engineers will help people like insects

DL 21　CD1-73

## Summary

**以下の a ～ d を本文に出てきた順番に合うように並べ替え、それぞれの Part の要約文を作りましょう。最後に音声を聞いて確認しましょう。**

Part 1

[　　] → [　　] → [　　] → [　　]

a. If you are to make insect foods popular, you must develop appealing dishes that promote people's appetite.

b. It was reported that powdered mealworms turned out to be an appetizing seasoning.

c. Although many people reject the idea of eating bugs, insects could be raised at a lower cost than common livestock.

d. Once a successful insect-based food gets publicity, other products might follow increasingly faster.

Part 2

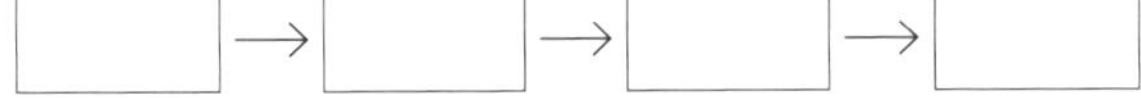

a. With the aid of engineering, we might be able to overcome what at first seems disgusting, a researcher says.

b. If you use ground-up insects, for example, the act of eating insects might become less unpleasant, scientists think.

c. Scientists directed their attention to cooking mealworms to know what recipe would create a meaty aroma.

d. Scientists in South Korea tried to cook mealworms in various ways—such as roasting, frying, or steaming.

## Writing Strategy

**日本語の意味に合うように [　　] 内の語 (句) を並べ替え、英文を完成させましょう。**

1. 科学者たちは、環境にやさしいたんぱく源としての昆虫の有益性に、スポットライトをあてた。
Scientists directed a spotlight on the usefulness of [ *an* / *as* / *environmentally* / *friendly* / *insects* / *of* / *protein* / *source* ].

______________________________________________

2. 昆虫由来の食品を食べるよう人々に勧めるためには、食欲をそそるような香りを出せるかどうかが重要になる。
Whether or not [ *appetizing* / *can* / *foods* / *give off* / *insect-based* / *aromas* ] is key to inviting people to eat them.

______________________________________________

## Clue to Usage

### 便利な動名詞

このユニットには動名詞を含む構文が多用されている。２つの種類があり、１つは動名詞を主語にしたもので、Part 1ではAdding (ℓ. 3)とFinding (ℓ. 16)があり、Part 2にはSteaming (ℓ. 33)、Roasting and frying (ℓ. 33)、Using (ℓ. 40)がある。２つ目は前置詞の目的語になっているもので、Part 1ではin chomping down (ℓ. 12) や、to getting them (ℓ. 18)、またPart 2ではabout eating insects (ℓ. 41) や with eating insects (ℓ. 43) に見られる。ところでFinding out how to make insect-based foods more appetizing could be key to getting them into more kitchens ... (ℓ. 16)のような文は、主語が長く、読みづらい。その場合は、If you find out ... it could be key ～ などと書き換えると、意味が取りやすくなる。

### for oneの意味

She, for one, has no problem with eating insects. (ℓ. 42) は「彼女自身としては、昆虫食には何ら抵抗はない」という意味にとれるが、これはother people may not agree with me, but at least in my opinion, ... といった彼女の気持ちを表している。
一方、次の文の場合は、「いくつか問題点があるが、一例をあげると」という意味にとる。
ex) There are some problems with eating insects. Mealworms, for one, are lacking in flavor.

## Approaching the Contents

**質問文の下線部分を書き取り、解答をａ～ｄから選びましょう。**

Q: According to the author, what could ______________________ the popularization of insect-based food?

a. Finding out how to key in on increasing the amount of protein in them.
b. Trying various methods of grinding pieces of insects into powder.
c. Making insect-based food more appetizing so that people approve of it.
d. Offering more delicious dishes as an alternative to insects.

Q: How did the scientists try to produce an aroma that resembles ______________________ meat and seafood?

a. By rating which scent is more fragrant of the two.
b. By drying insects thoroughly before cooking.
c. By steaming insects so that they retain their original shapes.
d. By roasting and frying the larvae of darkling beetles.

# Over to you!

以下の表は食用に適した昆虫の紹介です。1～7に適切な語（句）を語群から選び、コメント欄の英文を完成させましょう。必要に応じて語形は変えること。

| Insect | Where in the world? | Nutrition information | Ways of eating |
|---|---|---|---|
| Crickets | Crickets, one of the best-known (1. ) insects, are particularly popular in Laos and Thailand. | Serv. Size: 100 grams<br>Calories: 121<br>Total Fat: 5.5 grams<br>Protein: 20.5 grams | Crickets are commonly dry-roasted, made into flours, or eaten whole in salads. Dessert foods can (2. ) be made with them. |
| Ants | People in Colombia (3. ) several Asian countries, including Cambodia, eat ants. | Serv. Size: 100 grams<br>Calories: 83<br>Total Fat: 3.5 grams<br>Protein: 13.9 grams | Try toasting ants dry with salt and (4. ) seasoning. Or make a sweet treat by covering the with chocolate. |
| Mealworms | Mealworms are a favorite food (5. ). People in the Netherlands, in particular, enjoy this tasty food. | Serv. Size: 100 grams<br>Calories: 223<br>Total Fat: 7.2 grams<br>Protein: 23.7 grams | People can enjoy mealworms by having them fried or (6. ) them whole, or making them into bread. |
| Termites | Termites are great food in some parts of African countries and Indonesia. | Serv. Size: 100 grams<br>Calories: 221<br>Total Fat: n/a<br>Protein: 14.2 grams | Use palm (7. ) to fry termites or enjoy them dry roasted. |



also　as well as　eating　edible　oil　vinegar　worldwide

# Unit 8

# Deep-Sea Floor Microbes

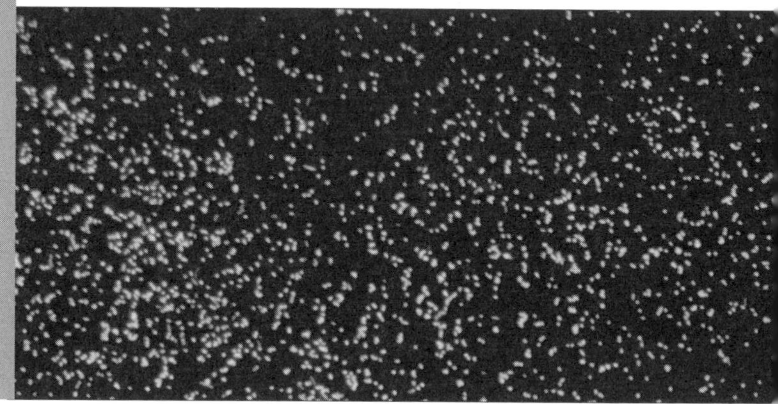

## 1億年の眠りから覚めた微生物

南太平洋の海底にある堆積物から1億年以上生きている微生物が発見されました。ただ発見されただけではありません。「エサ」を与えると待ちかねたように食べ出し、猛烈なスピードで繁殖を始めたのです。生命の不思議を解き明かすヒントを求め、タイムプセルから取り出されたような微生物相手の研究が加速します。

## Word Choice

**日本語の意味に合うように a ～ f から適切な語を選びましょう。ただし、選択肢には解答と関係のないものもあります。**

1

| | |
|---|---|
| 1. 人生の意味をじっくり考える | (　　　　) the meaning of life |
| 2. 感謝祭のごちそうを楽しむ | enjoy a Thanksgiving (　　　　) |
| 3. 膨大な量のデータを収集する | collect a (　　　　) amount of data |
| 4. ハリケーン多発地域を避けて住む | avoid living in a hurricane-prone (　　　　) |
| 5. 赤道直下の国々を訪ねる | visit the countries right on the (　　　　) |

a. equator　b. feast　c. ponder　d. region　e. sediment　f. vast

2

| | |
|---|---|
| 1. 上質なたんぱく質を含む | (　　　　) high-quality protein |
| 2. 販売報告書に詳細な分析が欠けていることに言及する | (　　　　) the lack of detailed analysis in the sales report |
| 3. 民族的に多様な社会に暮らす | live in an ethnically (　　　　) society |
| 4. 窒素肥料を毎日与える | spread some nitrogen-based (　　　　) on a daily basis |
| 5. コロナ後の観光産業をよみがえらせる | (　　　　) the tourism industry post-COVID-19 |

a. contain　b. cubic　c. diverse　d. fertilizer　e. note　f. revive

DL 23 CD1-75 ~ CD1-86

## Reading

### Some deep-seafloor microbes are still alive after 100 million years!

Part 1

Some bacteria give new meaning to the word old. After sleeping many, many, *many* years beneath the seafloor, scientists woke them up. How long had they been resting? Try more than 100 million years! No surprise, these cells were really ready for breakfast.

Scientists have pondered how long energy-starved seafloor microbes might survive. There certainly had been signs that it could be a million years or more. Some researchers now just got a chance to test that. They collected sediments dating back 13 million to nearly 102 million years. Nearly all of the microbes inside these samples were dormant. They appeared to be resting quietly.

Just like Sleeping Beauty, they were waiting to be wakened. And it was done not with the kiss of a prince but with a breakfast feast. Offered food, even the oldest of these microbes woke back up and began reproducing. Researchers in Japan shared their discovery on July 28 in *Nature Communications*.

These findings show life can exist even in very extreme environments. No food? That's okay. These patient cells will just wait. And wait. And wait. When the food truck finally arrives, they'll perk up, growing and multiplying.

These microbes had been living beneath a vast, flat, sediment-covered plain. It's essentially an ocean desert 3,700 to 5,700 meters (2.3 to 3.5 miles) beneath the sea surface.

Yuki Morono is a microbiologist. He works for the Japan Agency for Marine-Earth Science and Technology in Kochi. Morono and his team worked with sediments collected in 2010. They came from beneath the South Pacific Gyre. Earth's oceans host five major gyres; each is a large region of rotating ocean currents. The newfound deep-sea microbes came from under a Pacific gyre south of the equator.

Notes

energy-starved エネルギー不足の

sediment 堆積物

dormant 眠っている

Sleeping Beauty 眠れる森の美女

began reproducing 生殖行動を開始した

*Nature Communications* 自然科学の全分野を広く扱うオンラインジャーナル

perk up 旺盛に活動する

multiplying 増殖する

plain 平らな場所

microbiologist 微生物学者

Japan Agency for Marine-Earth Science and Technology 国立研究開発法人海洋研究開発機構 (JAMSTEC)

South Pacific Gyre 南太平洋環流

Part 2

Waters in the gyre contain few nutrients. So the phytoplankton that can feed a cascade of ocean life doesn't bloom here. The result: Almost no organic matter — food — filters down through the water. That leaves the ocean floor below a nutrient desert.

Any organisms here will not be happy campers. "Microbes that are unfortunate enough to find themselves there are destined to starve for a long, long time," noted Craig Moyer, back in 2015. Moyer is a biologist at Western Washington University in Bellingham. There he specializes in the ecology of ocean microbes.

The extremely slow collection of organic material and other sediments below a gyre does allow oxygen in the water to seep deep into the sediment. Morono and his colleagues wondered if this oxygen might allow aerobic, or oxygen-loving, microbes in the sediment to hang on, waiting for their next meal.

To find out, they "fed" carbon, nitrogen, and more — fertilizers, really — to the microbes in these sediments. The aerobic microbes turned out to be a highly diverse group. They were mostly different bacteria from a few large groups. Among these groups were alpha and gamma proteobacteria. Those family names may sound odd, but their members include some commonly known types. Among them are enterobacteria (of which *E. coli* and *Salmonella* are members) and the *Vibrio* bacteria that have gained renown for causing shellfish poisonings.

Nearly all the long-dormant microbes responded quickly to the food. By 68 days after the start of the experiment, their numbers had skyrocketed from as few as several 100 cells per cubic centimeter to 1 million cells per cubic centimeter.

And not just microbes from the youngest sediments woke up and became active. Even in the sample with the most elderly microbes — ones some 101.5 million years old — feeding revived up to 99.1 percent of them.

(590 words)

phytoplankton 植物性プランクトン

Western Washington University ウェスタン・ワシントン大学。ワシントン州ベリンガムにある公立大学。1893年設立。

seep 染み込む

aerobic 好気性の

alpha and gamma proteobacteria アルファプロテオバクテリア綱とガンマプロテオバクテリア綱（プロテオバクテリアは細菌の門のひとつ）

*E.coli* 大腸菌
*Salmonella* サルモネラ菌

had skyrocketed 急増した

cubic centimeter 1立方センチメートル

## Exercises

KEY PHRASES

(　　)に適切な語句を語群から選び英文を完成させましょう。ただし、必要に応じて語形は変えること。

1. Some stone bridges have histories (　　　　　　　　　　) to Roman times.
2. The baseball coach believed that the boy (　　　　　　　　　　) become a major leaguer.
3. The rising boy band always seemed (　　　　　　　　　　) attention from the audience.
4. I want to be a lawyer (　　　　　　　　　　) a juvenile law.
5. She (　　　　　　　　　　) to be as friendly a person as we thought she was.

| be destined to | date back | specialize in | starve for | turn out |
|---|---|---|---|---|

IN-DEPTH REVIEW

本文の内容に合うようにa～cから(　　)に適切な語句を選びましょう。

Part 1

1. When the scientists collected the sediments, (　　　　).
   a. there was no sign of organisms in them
   b. the microbes were not active
   c. some bacteria started reproducing
2. The microbes Morono collected (　　　　).
   a. had been living in the desert above a huge plain
   b. were residents of the gyre south of the equator
   c. proved the existence of five major gyres

Part 2

1. The sediments in the deep sea (　　　　).
   a. allow the campers to find food
   b. offer ideal conditions for organisms
   c. contain oxygen
2. The experiment showed that (　　　　) were alive and ready to eat.
   a. only newly discovered bacteria
   b. just a few familiar types of aerobic microbes
   c. even the microbes sleeping for over 100 million years

DL 24 CD1-87

## Summary

**以下の a ~ d を本文に出てきた順番に合うように並べ替え、それぞれの Part の要約文を作りましょう。最後に音声を聞いて確認しましょう。**

Part 1

[ ] → [ ] → [ ] → [ ]

a. The sediments containing microbes were sampled from under the South Pacific Gyre.

b. Even in very harsh environments, microbes can wait patiently for a day of revival.

c. Researchers have long wondered how long microbes can live without any food.

d. Scientists found out that even the oldest microbes can wake up if given food.

Part 2

[ ] → [ ] → [ ] → [ ]

a. Microbes in the sediments under the gyre were on the edge of dying from hunger.

b. You can scarcely find any organic material, including plankton, in the gyre.

c. Enough oxygen in the sediment may have enabled starving microbes to survive.

d. When they are fed nutrients, microbes quickly respond to the food, starting to reproduce.

## Writing Strategy

**日本語の意味に合うように [　　] 内の語を並べ替え、英文を完成させましょう。**

1. ひとたび宇宙船の外へ放り出されれば、ほぼすべての生物はたちまち死滅するだろう。
[ *all* / *almost* / *of* / *once* / *out* / *spaceship* / *a* / *thrown* ] organisms will die immediately.

______________________________

2. 最も厳しい冬の気象条件の下でさえ、この植物種はなおも生存することが可能だ。
[ *conditions* / *even* / *severest* / *the* / *under* / *weather* ] in winter, this plant species could still survive.

______________________________

## Clue to Usage

### 譲歩の最上級

even the oldest of these microbes woke back up (ℓ. 15) と、Even in the sample with the most elderly microbes (ℓ. 61) の表現は、ともに形容詞の最上級を含んでおり、「(新しい堆積層ならまだしも)最古の地層から出た微生物さえ復活する」という意味を表す。

ex) Even the strongest lion can be beaten by a small ant.「最強のライオンでさえ、小さなアリに負けかねない」

上の例のように、最上級が「たとえ最も～であってもなお」という譲歩を表すことがある。evenはつかないこともある。

### 分詞構文と接続詞

Turning to the right, you will find the Chinese restaurant.のような分詞構文を、接続詞を使った複文に戻すとき、If you turn to the right, you will find ... と考えることができる。上記でも取り上げたOffered food, even the oldest of these microbes woke back up ... (ℓ. 15) の場合なら、When they were offered food, ... と書き換えられる。

一方、they'll perk up, growing and multiplying (ℓ. 21) の場合は、内容に鑑みて等位接続詞を使うのが適切と思われるため、and grow and multiplyと解釈できる。to hang on, waiting (ℓ. 46) にも同じことが言え、to hang on and waitと解釈することができるが、ただ、こちらは従属接続詞を使って to hang on while (they are) waiting と書き換える方法も可能だ。

 DL 25  CD1-88

## Approaching the Contents

**質問文の下線部分を書き取り、解答をａ～ｄから選びましょう。**

Part 1

Q: What did the scientists find by doing tests on ______________________?

a. To their surprise, the collected sediments had many dormant organisms.
b. They learned that microbes survive extremely harsh environments for a long time.
c. They discovered the existence of rotating ocean currents for the first time.
d. They demonstrated that any food could work well for Sleeping Beauty.

Part 2

Q: What happened when microbes from gyre sediments ______________________?

a. Microbes from young sediments naturally did not enjoy the food at all.
b. Scientists found out that microbes preferred oxygen to other elements.
c. Not a microbe contained in the sediment was responsive to the meal.
d. Even the oldest microbes became awake and began to breed again.

# Over to you!

□ 内のそれぞれの海流に該当するものを、地図上のア～オから選び、記号で答えましょう。また、下に続く The South Pacific Gyre についての短い紹介文の [　　] に適切な語を Keywords から選び、英文を完成させましょう。ただし、必要に応じて語形は変えること。

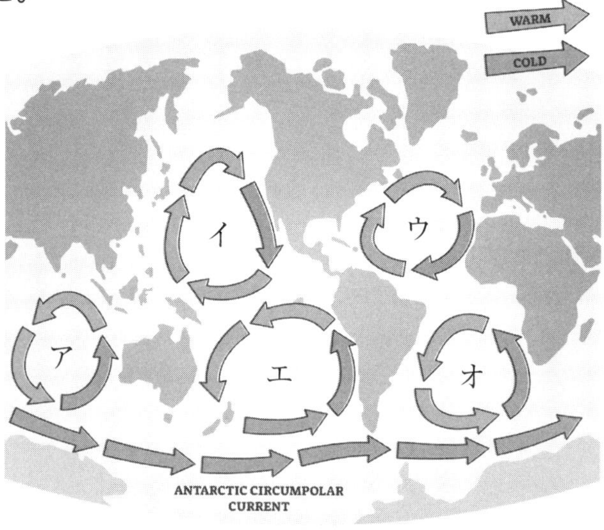


South Atlantic Gyre [　　　　] / North Atlantic Gyre [　　　　] / South Pacific Gyre [　　　　]
North Pacific Gyre [　　　　] / Indian Ocean Gyre [　　　　]

One of the five oceanic gyres in the global ocean is the South Pacific Gyre (SPG). A large system of circular ocean [　　　　] formed by global wind patterns and forces created by Earth's [　　　　] is called an ocean gyre. The SPG is not only the largest defined oceanic province on Earth, but also the most remote, located further from any continent than any other oceanic region. Almost 10% of our planet's ocean surface is covered by it, and it is distinguished by some of the [　　　　] water on Earth as well as several unique and extreme oceanographic properties. These properties include extremely [　　　　] nutrient content, which causes low productivity, and extremely low chlorophyll concentrations. The SPG has been referred to as a "biological [　　　　]" due to this combination of facts.

**Keywords** clear / current / desert / low / rotation

# Unit 9

# Wildfire and Air Pollution

## 命を脅かす 山火事の黒煙

焦土と化した森林や火傷を負った動物の姿は山火事の恐ろしさを伝えますが、カメラに映らない大気中の汚染物質、特にPM2.5として知られる微小粒子状物質もまた大きな脅威です。微小粒子状物質が及ぼす健康被害は呼吸器系の病気にとどまらず、心血管疾患の引き金ともなり、寿命を縮める要因となることが実証されました。

## Word Choice

**日本語の意味に合うように a ～ f から適切な語を選びましょう。ただし、選択肢には解答と関係のないものもあります。**

Part 1

| | |
|---|---|
| 1. 通常の寿命の２倍生きる | live up to two times longer than the normal ( ) |
| 2. 雨ざらしを避ける | prevent ( ) to rain |
| 3. おれおれ詐欺の証拠を集める | ( ) evidence of "it's me" fraud |
| 4. 潮力発電所建設計画を推進する | promote a plan to construct a tidal power ( ) |
| 5. 火山から黒煙がもうもうと立ち昇っているのを目撃する | witness a ( ) of black smoke rising from the volcano |

a. contain　b. exposure　c. gather　d. lifespan　e. station　f. plume

Part 2

| | |
|---|---|
| 1. 大陸移動説を参照する | refer to the ( ) drift theory |
| 2. 水だけでなんとか生き延びる | manage to survive on water ( ) |
| 3. 肝臓と腎臓に重大な影響を与える | profoundly ( ) the liver and kidneys |
| 4. 高齢化社会にとって重大な事柄を扱う | handle the ( ) issues of an aging society |
| 5. 睡眠薬の処方を厳しく規制する | strictly ( ) the prescription of sleeping pills |

a. affect　b. alone　c. continental　d. critical　e. regulate　f. routinely

## Reading

### *Wildfires are pumping more pollution into U.S. skies*

*Part 1*

Notes

In parts of the western United States, sometimes the sky looks gray and the sun is hidden from view. Not because of clouds but because of wildfire smoke. That smoke contains tiny particles, which are harmful to health. Now, researchers have found that exposure to such pollution has grown in the United States over the past decade as wildfires have gotten bigger and more common.

"There are so many health effects from particulate matter," or PM, says Marissa Childs. As an environmental health researcher, she works at Harvard University in Cambridge, Mass. Especially concerning are really small particles, called PM2.5. These are smaller than 2.5 micrometers. That's about one-thirty-fifth the thickness of a sheet of paper.

Health risks from such particles include asthma and shorter lifespans. Childs and her colleagues wanted to better understand the health effects of PM2.5 from wildfire smoke. But first, they needed to know how much exposure to it people in different places were having. So, the researchers set out to map this pollution.

First, they gathered data on PM2.5 levels from about 2,000 air-monitoring stations across the United States. Satellite images of plumes of wildfire smoke allowed the researchers to estimate how much of the PM2.5 in each place appeared to come from this smoke.

particulate matter 微粒子状物質

Cambridge, Mass. マサチューセッツ州ケンブリッジ

2.5 micrometers 2.5マイクロメーター(1マイクロメーターは1メートルの100万分の1)

asthma 喘息

*Part 2*

Vast areas, however, have no monitoring stations. To estimate smoke PM2.5 in those places, Childs' team started with satellite images of smoke plumes. Then they trained a computer model to calculate smoke PM2.5 levels based partly on those images. The model considered many factors, including wind direction and speeds, temperature, and distance to the

trained ～に教え込んだ

fire.

This allowed the team to estimate the daily PM2.5 from smoke to which people across the continental United States were exposed from 2006 to 2020. (The map did not include Alaska or Hawaii.)

"We especially see a really large increase in the number of extreme days with high pollution levels," says Childs. In 2020 alone, 25 million people experienced at least one day where PM2.5 levels were over 100 micrograms per cubic meter. On days with such high pollution, people in affected areas shouldn't spend a lot of time outside.

100 micrograms 100マイクログラム(1マイクログラムは100万分の1グラム)
per cubic meter 1立方メートル当たり

The researchers shared their findings in the October 4 *Environmental Science & Technology*.

"It is time that we start treating wildfires like a critical social problem," says Childs. Particle pollution from smoke isn't regulated under U.S. clean-air laws. That "might have made sense 10 years ago, when wildfires were exceptional," Childs says. Now, there are places that routinely experience unhealthy levels of particles from wildfires. "We can't think of them as exceptional anymore."

(428 words)

*Further Notes*

ℓ.10 **Harvard University** マサチューセッツ州ケンブリッジに本部を置くアメリカ最古の大学。1636 年創立。長年にわたって世界のトップランクに位置する名門大学のひとつ。

ℓ.43 ***Environmental Science & Technology*** アメリカ化学会が発行する環境に関連する科学技術を扱う国際的学術雑誌。環境に直接かかわるエネルギーと気候、環境汚染、環境における持続可能なシステムなど、広範囲なトピックを扱う。

ℓ.46 **U.S. clean-air laws** 大気浄化法（Clean Air Act）のこと。従来は地域や州に任されていた大気汚染の全米規模での防止を目的に 1963 年に制定された法律。制定後、産業構造の高度化に伴い 1970 年、1977 年、1990 年に改正が行われ、その都度、対象とされる問題が拡大し、現在に至っている。当初からの目的である大気汚染の防止以外の内容としては、酸性雨対策、オゾン層の保護、自動車による排ガス削減などが含まれる。

## Exercises

KEY PHRASES

(　　)に適切な語句を語群から選び英文を完成させましょう。ただし、必要に応じて語形は変えること。

1. Our leader (　　　　　　　　　　) to rearrange the financial plan.
2. Brilliant ideas often (　　　　　　　　　　) casual conversations.
3. Let me (　　　　　　　　　　) an introduction of the history of our factory.
4. Her theory (　　　　　　　　　　) live experiments in the lab.
5. The first thing I (　　　　　　　　　　) when I visited the castle was the power of the king.

| be based on | come from | set out | start with | think of |
|---|---|---|---|---|

IN-DEPTH REVIEW

本文の内容に合うようにa～cから(　　)に適切な語句を選びましょう。

t1

1. The particles in wildfire smoke (　　　　).
   a. are detected across the United States
   b. are hidden by the sun
   c. are relevant to human health problem
2. In order to understand the influence of PM2.5 on health, the team (　　　　).
   a. conducted systematic research on small particles from wildfire smoke
   b. counted the number of people exposed to the smoke
   c. monitored the scale of wildfire from the 2,000 satellites

t2

1. As (　　　　), the researchers started to use satellite images.
   a. it was hard to program a computer model to calculate the smoke
   b. some monitoring stations were in trouble
   c. the research area was too large
2. According to Childs, (　　　　).
   a. wildfires are not as exceptional as they used to be
   b. wildfires cause only a few people to be affected by harmful particles
   c. high pollution prevented 25 million Americans from going out in 2020

DL 27 CD2-11

## Summary

**以下の a ～ d を本文に出てきた順番に合うように並べ替え、それぞれの Part の要約文を作りましょう。最後に音声を聞いて確認しましょう。**

Part 1

□ → □ → □ → □

a. As a first step, researchers drew up a map showing PM2.5 pollution.

b. Wildfire smoke contains particles that are bad for the health.

c. Thanks to satellite images, researchers could understand how wildfires and PM2.5 are related.

d. They paid attention to extremely small pieces of matter—smaller than 0.0025mm.

Part 2

a. Childs insists that we should regard wildfires as an extremely dangerous problem.

b. Using satellite images, the researchers analyzed PM2.5 levels with a computer model.

c. Researchers found that the number of extremely polluted days was increasing in the U.S.

d. Scientists warn that pollution by wildfires may not be a rare occasion.

## Writing Strategy

**日本語の意味に合うように [　　] 内の語を並べ替え、英文を完成させましょう。**

1. もうそろそろ、研究者が新型コロナウイルス感染症の治療薬を開発してもよい頃だ。
[ *an* / *developed* / *drug* / *effective* / *is* / *it* / *researchers* / *time* ] to treat COVID-19.

______________________________

2. ジェニファーはまだ 25 歳だったが、人々は彼女を経験豊かな看護師だと考えていた。
Jennifer was only 25 years old, but people [ *an* / *as* / *experienced* / *her* / *nurse* / *of* / *thought* ].

______________________________

## Clue to Usage

### It is time ... の構文

It is time that we start treating wildfires like a critical social problem. (ℓ. 44) は「～を始める頃合い／～すべき時だ」という意味でとれる。この文は、startをstartedにして仮定法過去としてもよい。仮定法を使わない簡単な表現もある。

ex) It is time that you went to bed.「そろそろ君は寝るべき時間ではないか」

shouldを使う：It is time (that) you should go to bed now.

to不定詞を使う（文型を変える）：Now, it is time for you to go to bed.

### regard A as Bの類型

regard A as B「AをBと見なす」のようにasを使う動詞として、class, define, describeなどがある。例えば以下のような文。

ex) The company classed him as a part-time worker. / Her friends described Diane as kind and generous.

さらに、We can't think of them as exceptional anymore. (ℓ. 49)「もはや例外だとは見なしえない」のようにthink of ～やlook on ～などの句動詞の後にasがくる場合もある。

ex) Jane has always looked on him as a friend.

上の文は、Jane has always considered him to be a friend.と書き換えられるが、この文のconsider や elect, count などの動詞はasの他にto be～とつなぐこともできる。

DL 28 CD2-12

## Approaching the Contents

**質問文の下線部分を書き取り、解答をa～dから選びましょう。**

1 Q: Why did Childs think it necessary to know ________________ wildfire smoke?

a. Because the team needed to detect the smallest possible particles in the clouds.
b. Because the urgent task she was faced with was how to cure serious diseases.
c. Because she was particularly concerned about particles of bigger sizes.
d. Because such data was essential to examine how people's health is affected by the smoke.

2 Q: According to Childs, something ________________________ 10 years ago. What does she mean?

a. In those days, scientists witnessed many days with high pollution levels.
b. Ten years ago, regulations to control particle pollution did not seem necessary.
c. Many scientists did not regard wildfires as exceptional.
d. Satellite images of smoke have become available only recently.

# Over to you!

**以下はオーストラリアの Rachel からアメリカのカリフォルニア州の Tim へ送られたメールです。[　　] に適切な語を Keywords から選び、提示されているクイズにも答えましょう。**

**Keywords** added / destroyed / hit / reserved

Dear Tim,

The story of wildfires (Unit 9) was quite alarming. In Australia, too, a wide region has been [　　　　　] by bushfires near Sydney in recent years. You may not know this, but wildfires or forest fires are generally called bushfires here in Australia.
The bushfires in 2019-2020 were a most devastating disaster, killing at least 33 people as direct victims of scorching fire. [　　　　　] to this figure, an estimated 445 people died not on the spot but later due to fire-related reasons. Now Tim, can you guess *what the exact cause of their later deaths was*?
The bushfire was also a terrible disaster for wildlife. Unlike the outback—mostly inland arid plane—the bush is connected to the mountain areas and is a major habitat for wild animals. Reportedly, some 3 billion animals—mammals, reptiles, and birds—were killed or harmed, including the familiar kangaroos and koalas. It is deplorable that their vast habitats [　　　　　].
See you soon. Please remember to answer my quiz.
Rachel

Which is the correct answer to the question mentioned above?

**(1)** They died from respiratory diseases due to ultrafine particles inhaled when they were exposed to the bushfire smoke.

**(2)** While running away from the blazing fire, many people were injured or burnt, which led to deadly infectious diseases.

**(3)** It was an extreme shortage of drinking water and food as well as medical supplies that caused their early deaths.

# Unit 10

# Spiders — Unfair Negative Image

### クモはフェイクニュースの犠牲者

科学の領域にはクモを専門に研究をしている科学者もいます。長年、クモは不快昆虫だと言われてきました。しかし、研究者たちの科学的な証明によって、クモに対するその汚名が晴らされるかもしれません。証明の裏付けとなるのは、過去にさかのぼって調べ上げられた、フェイクニュースの数々です。

## Word Choice

**日本語の意味に合うように a ～ f から適切な語を選びましょう。ただし、選択肢には解答と関係のないものもあります。**

1

| | |
|---|---|
| 1. 道で旧友に出くわす | (　　　　) an old friend on the street |
| 2. くっきりと三分割した細胞 | a cell (　　　　) divided into three parts |
| 3. すべてを他人のせいにする | (　　　　) others for everything |
| 4. 医師に症状を報告する | report a (　　　　) to the doctor |
| 5. 理論を事実に合わせる | let the theory (　　　　) the fact |

a. actual　b. blame　c. distinctly　d. encounter　e. match　f. symptom

2

| | |
|---|---|
| 1. 敗北の苦しみから立ち直る | recover from the (　　　　) of defeat |
| 2. 無農薬野菜を栽培する | grow (　　　　)-free vegetables |
| 3. 戦場で有毒な神経ガスを検出する | detect (　　　　) nerve gas on the battlefield |
| 4. 発酵食品で免疫を高める | (　　　　) immunity by eating fermented food |
| 5. 駐独大使を任命する | appoint an (　　　　) to Germany |

a. ambassador　b. agony　c. boost　d. pesticide　e. regional　f. toxic

DL 29 CD2-13 ~ CD2-22

## Reading

### New stories about spiders are unfairly negative

*Part 1*

Spiders are pretty remarkable. They live almost everywhere, from rainforests to deserts. Some even spend most of their lives underwater. They are smarter than you think, with some able to make plans and count. Scientists think they might even dream when they sleep. Yet many people find these eight-legged animals creepy or scary. Now, it seems, fake news may be partly to blame. Media reports about people's encounters with spiders tend to be full of falsehoods, a new study finds. Researchers analyzed a decade's worth of newspaper stories. These articles were published in dozens of countries. Nearly half contained errors. And those untruths about spiders had a distinctly negative spin.

Researchers shared the findings on August 22 in *Current Biology*.

"The vast majority of the spider content out there is about them being scary and hurting people," says Catherine Scott. In reality, they note, "spiders almost never bite people." An arachnologist, Scott studies spiders at McGill University in Montreal, Canada.

Of some 50,000 species of spiders known to science, only a few are dangerous. In fact, many spiders protect us by eating insects, such as mosquitoes, that spread disease. Even spiders that could pose a threat — such as the brown recluse and the black widow — rarely bite people, Scott says.

But error-filled news reports paint spiders in a different light. Some stories about spider bites blamed species that don't even live where the bite happened. Others reported that people bitten by spiders showed symptoms that don't match those of actual bites. In fact, Scott found, "Many stories about spider bites included no evidence whatsoever that there was any spider involved."

Notes

with some able to ~ 中には~できるもの(=クモ)も含まれている
creepy 気味の悪い
falsehood 偽り
a decade's worth of ~ 10年分の~
dozens of ~ 多数の~
negative spin マイナスにひねった解釈
out there そこの、そこにある
arachnologist クモ学者
pose a threat 脅威を与える
brown recluse ドクイトグモ
black widow クロゴケグモ
no evidence whatsoever いかなる証拠もいっさいない(…で)ない

Part 2

For the new study, Scott and their colleagues analyzed more than 5,000 online newspaper stories about humans and spiders. Each had been published between 2010 and 2020. They came from 81 countries and were written in 40 languages.

The researchers didn't just find errors in the stories. More than four in every 10 articles had sensationalized the spiders' behaviors. Such overblown stories often used words like *nasty, killer*, *agony* and *nightmare* to describe the arachnids. International and national newspapers were more likely to use sensational terms than were regional outlets. Stories that included a spider expert were less sensational. That was not true for stories that quoted other types of experts, such as doctors.

overblown 誇張された
nasty 不快な
arachnid クモ形類動物
outlet 新聞社

If people knew the truth about spiders, they would spend less time blaming them for bites caused by other animals, Scott argues. People might also be less likely to kill spiders with pesticides that are toxic to other species (including humans).

Clearing spiders' name would be good for them, too. (Say, for instance, the one in your house that doesn't get squashed out of fear.)

say たとえば
get squashed つぶされる

Improving spiders' public image could even boost conservation efforts in general. "Spiders are kind of unique in that they seem to be really good at capturing people's attention," says Lisa Taylor. This arachnologist at the University of Florida in Gainesville was not involved in the study. "If that attention is paired with real information about how fascinating they are ... then I think spiders are well-suited to serve as tiny ambassadors for wildlife in general."

conservation effort 自然保護の努力
is paired with ～ ～と一組になる

(523 words)

## *Further Notes*

ℓ.13 ***Current Biology*** カレントバイオロジー。1991年に刊行されたアメリカの学術誌。生物学全般を扱い、隔週で発行される。

ℓ.18 **McGill University** マギル大学。1821年創立のカナダでもっとも歴史の古い大学。本部をケベック州モントリオールに置く。

ℓ.54 **University of Florida** フロリダ大学。フロリダ州ゲインズビルに本部をかまえる州立大学。フロリダ州で最も歴史が古く、最大規模の大学。

## Exercises

KEY PHRASES　(　　)に適切な語句を語群から選び英文を完成させましょう。ただし、必要に応じて語形は変えること。

1. The fire caused $300,000 (　　　　　　　　　　) damage to the houses in the area.
2. Many reporters asked (　　　　　　　　　　) questions to the Prime Minister.
3. The current debate is whether or not AI (　　　　　　　　　　) humanity.
4. In the last lesson, students (　　　　　　　　　　) partners to practice the dialogue.
5. The summit of this mountain (　　　　　　　　　　) astronomical observations.

| be paired with | be suited to | dozens of | pose a threat to | worth of |
|---|---|---|---|---|

IN-DEPTH REVIEW　本文の内容に合うようにa～cから(　　)に適切な語句を選びましょう。

Part 1

1. The researchers examined (　　　　) and found myriad untruths about spiders.
   a. eight-legged creatures
   b. the news published in the twelve countries
   c. ten years' worth of newspaper stories
2. Catherine Scott points out that (　　　　).
   a. the content of few articles is misleading
   b. many spiders are beneficial to humans
   c. a black widow bites humans quite often

Part 2

1. Scott's team found that (　　　　).
   a. less than a quarter of the news stories in their research are fake
   b. spider behavior is exaggerated in some articles
   c. spider experts overused sensational terms to warn people
2. Lisa Taylor suggests that (　　　　).
   a. spiders will lead us to better understand nature
   b. conservation efforts are necessary to improve people's image of spiders
   c. we need to train spiders to serve as small ambassadors

DL 30 CD2-23

## Summary

**以下の a ～ d を本文に出てきた順番に合うように並べ替え、それぞれの Part の要約文を作りましょう。最後に音声を聞いて確認しましょう。**

t 1

a. Reportedly, spiders are intelligent creatures that in some cases may be able to make plans and count.

b. As a matter of fact, spiders are beneficial to human life because they eat harmful insects like mosquitoes.

c. After examining a decade's worth of newspaper reports on spiders, researchers found that many contained false information.

d. Some people insist that they were bitten by spiders, though their symptoms indicate otherwise.

t 2

a. One scientist says that real knowledge about how fascinating spiders are needs to be shared.

b. If you were to set the record straight about spiders, it would be helpful to their welfare and, by extension, to the environment in general.

c. Analysis by the scientists showed not only factual errors in the stories but also some exaggerated wording.

d. It turned out that regional newspapers used less sensational terms when describing spiders than big mass media.

## Writing Strategy

**日本語の意味に合うように [　　] 内の語を並べ替え、英文を完成させましょう。**

1. 汚職に対する警察の捜査は、しかし、事務総長が関与していたといういかなる証拠も提示することはなかった。
The police investigation into corruption, however, [ *evidence* / *gave* / *no* / *Secretary-General* / *that* / *the* / *whatsoever* ] had been involved.

2. もし私が早期に嫌疑を晴らしていたならば、こんな苦難は起こらなかっただろうに。
If I [ *charge* / *cleared* / *had* / *been* / *of* / *the* ] earlier, hardship like this wouldn't have happened.

## Clue to Usage

### blameのいろいろな使い方

このユニットにはblameという動詞が以下の３回登場する。

① spider bites blamed species (ℓ. 26) は「クモの種をとがめる」と意味を取ることができる。

② spend less time blaming them for bites (ℓ. 44) は、for bitesで「咬み傷の責任ゆえに」と理由を示してクモを非難する表現だ。この部分は語順を変えて、blaming bites on them「咬み傷の責任を彼らに向ける」のようにon を使って表現もできる。

③ fake news may be partly to blame. (ℓ. 6) は、be ... to blameの部分が異色の用法であり、この部分は「捏造ニュースに一部責任がある」と意味を取れる。

### 仮定法構文のIf節

以下の２例のように、仮定法構文に見えない場合、if節を補って考えてみると、文意が明瞭になる。

Clearing spiders' name would be good for them, too. (ℓ. 48)

→If you cleared spiders' name, it would be good for them, too.

Improving spiders' public image could even boost conservation efforts in general. (ℓ. 51)

→If spiders' public image were improved, it could even boost conservation efforts in general.

## Approaching the Contents

**質問文の下線部分を書き取り、解答をａ～ｄから選びましょう。**

Part 1

Q: If you say that a news ______________________, what does that mean?

a. It says the article's contents are reliable enough.
b. It refers to the article's biased way of looking at things.
c. It means that the author's viewpoint is easy to understand.
d. It suggests that the article has some major defects.

Part 2

Q: Why shouldn't you carelessly ______________________________?

a. Because many other species in nature may be killed, too.
b. Because they are not permitted in urban areas.
c. Because some experts recommend less dangerous chemicals.
d. Because they are not expected to kill harmful insects.

# Over to you!

1～4 はクモに関する FAQ です。質問に対する回答を (a) ～ (d) から選びましょう。また、[　　]に適切な語を Keywords から選び、(a) ～ (d) の英文を完成させましょう。

**FAQs**

1. Can spiders jump? (　　)
2. Are there any vegetarian spiders? (　　)
3. Do all spiders have eight eyes? (　　)
4. What is spider silk made of? (　　)

**Answers**

**Keywords** | **1.** leaves / **2.** components / **3.** predator / **4.** shadows

(a) It is made of connected and unconnected chains of liquid proteins whose chemical [　　　] vary depending on the types of function the spider's silk performs. The acidic nature of spider silk prevents bacteria or fungi from attacking it, allowing it to remain in the environment for many years.

(b) It has been found that at least one species living in Central America is mostly vegetarian. The trees that produce protein-rich buds on their [　　　] are where the spiders live. They exist by consuming the buds.

(c) It depends on the species. The majority of them have eight eyes, but some only have six. Spiders usually have a primary set that can create images, while the secondary sets are capable of detecting only light and [　　　].

(d) Some spiders can move very quickly and jump multiple times their body length when hunting or trying to escape from a [　　　]. Jumping spiders, for instance, are able to jump up to fifty times their own length.

# Unit 11

# Might Toothpaste Cure Allergies?

## 生活習慣を利用したアレルギー治療

ピーナッツアレルギーは、微量のピーナッツを長期間、定期的に摂取することで体内に耐性を作る治療法が多いですが、患者にとっては大きな負担となっています。安全性を担保した上で患者の負担を減らす治療法が、患者の多いアメリカで発表されました。日常生活の中に無理なく治療を組み込むための仕掛けがユニークです。

## Word Choice

**日本語の意味に合うようにａ～ｆから適切な語を選びましょう。ただし、選択肢には解答と関係のないものもあります。**

### Part 1

| | | |
|---|---|---|
| 1. | 薬物への耐性を獲得する | develop a (　　　　) to a drug |
| 2. | 既存の税制に異議を唱える | challenge the (　　　　) tax system |
| 3. | 誤って異物を飲みこむ | accidentally (　　　　) a foreign object |
| 4. | しかるべきコンピュータ技術を獲得する | acquire (　　　　) computer skills |
| 5. | 国境に永続的な平和をもたらす | bring (　　　　) peace to the border |

**a.** decent　**b.** durable　**c.** existing　**d.** swallow　**e.** tolerance　**f.** trigger

### Part 2

| | | |
|---|---|---|
| 1. | 内気な学生に勇気を起こさせる | (　　　　) courage in the shy students |
| 2. | 著名な弁護士に特許について相談する | consult a famous (　　　　) for advice on patents |
| 3. | 地元民とウェブサイトを共同で立ち上げる | (　　　　) a website with local people |
| 4. | のどのヒリヒリする痛みに苦しむ | suffer from a (　　　　) throat |
| 5. | タンパク質をほとんど含まない | (　　　　) almost no protein |

**a.** attorney　**b.** cofound　**c.** contain　**d.** gums　**e.** inspire　**f.** sore

DL 32 CD2-25 ~ CD2-33

## Reading

### *Could a toothpaste help treat peanut allergy?*

Part 1

Notes

It may one day be possible for people to treat food allergies by simply brushing their teeth. A New York City-based company has launched a trial of a product to do that in a small group of adults. All are allergic to peanuts. The idea is to expose users to small daily doses of peanut protein. That should help them to build and maintain tolerance to it.

tolerance 耐性

Tying this treatment to a daily routine should help allergy sufferers keep up with regular treatment, say researchers at Intrommune Therapeutics. The company developed the new toothpaste. This product may also do a better job than existing therapies, they add, at delivering the active ingredients in those treatments to immune cells throughout the mouth.

active ingredient 有効成分
immune cell 免疫細胞

Some 32 million Americans have food allergies. One existing treatment is oral immunotherapy. It exposes patients daily to small amounts of an allergen through doses swallowed as food. An allergen is a material, often a protein, that triggers allergic reactions. However, sometimes people react to this treatment itself. And tolerance to an allergen often wanes without maintenance dosing.

oral immunotherapy 経口免疫療法

wanes 弱まる

A gentler treatment is sublingual immunotherapy. It delivers smaller doses through liquid drops placed under the tongue. This therapy offers decent protection. It also causes fewer side effects. And it may be especially effective with allergies that are caught early. For instance, mouth drops produce stronger, more durable benefits in toddlers than in older children. Researchers reported this on February 27. They shared their discovery at a virtual meeting of the American Academy of Allergy, Asthma & Immunology.

sublingual immunotherapy 舌下免疫療法

toddler 幼児

Part 2

Still, it can be hard for patients to keep up with this daily therapy. And the immune cells thought to be the best target are not just under the tongue. They are actually densest inside the cheeks and elsewhere in the mouth.

William Reisacher is an allergist. He works at Weill Cornell Medicine in New York City. Several years ago, he was standing in front of a mirror brushing his teeth. "I saw all the foam in my mouth going into all the areas I wanted it to go," he says. And that inspired the idea of putting food proteins in toothpaste. This would get the treatment to the right cells *and* embed it in a routine daily habit.

"Bill told me this crazy idea he had, and I thought it was genius," says Michael Nelson. He's an attorney trained in biology and health care. He cofounded Intrommune to develop the toothpaste. The company just launched a clinical trial of the toothpaste that will enroll 32 adults who are allergic to peanuts. This trial will test how well they tolerate escalating doses of the allergen. Future trials may test toothpastes that contain several allergens, Nelson says.

Other allergists support the toothpaste concept. Some worry, however, about dose control and safety. Someone's gums can become sore and inflamed. This can happen, for example, after dental work or losing a tooth. Those inflamed gums might let allergens have direct access to the bloodstream. That could increase the risk of body-wide allergic reactions, says Sakina Bajowala. She's an allergist at Kaneland Allergy & Asthma Center in North Aurora, Ill. She offers oral and sublingual immunotherapies for food and environmental allergies.

"Safety is something I'm going to be watching closely," she says. But if "they can prove it's safe and effective," she says, "then fantastic."

(558 words)

allergist アレルギー専門医
embed 組み込む
trained in ～ ～を学んだ
cofounded ～を共同設立した
enroll ～を参加させる
escalating 程度や量が増してくる
gums 歯茎
inflamed 炎症を起こした

*Further Notes*

ℓ.9 **Intrommune Therapeutics** 安全かつ簡素化されたアレルギー免疫療法の開発に力を入れるバイオテクノロジー企業。2015 年に設立され、ニューヨーク市に本社を置く。

ℓ.27 **American Academy of Allergy, Asthma & Immunology** 米国アレルギー喘息免疫学会。アレルギー専門医、免疫学者などを主な構成員とし、アレルギー性疾患、喘息、免疫疾患の研究と治療を中心に活動する国際組織。ウィスコンシン州ミルウォーキーに本部を置く。

ℓ.54 **Kaneland Allergy & Asthma Center** アレルギー性疾患と免疫疾患の治療に注力する専門機関。2011 年に設立。イリノイ州ノース・オーロラに位置する。

## Exercises

**KEY PHRASES** ( )に適切な語句を語群から選び英文を完成させましょう。ただし、必要に応じて語形は変えること。

1. As his income declined, he wasn't able to ( ) the payment.
2. A recent study showed that art therapy ( ) young teenagers.
3. As I used to ( ) caffeine, I always preferred fruit juice to coffee.
4. The expedition party avoided ( ) the cave.
5. She is a nurse ( ) psychology at college.
6. Some insects ( ) their predators by emitting poisonous chemicals.

| be effective with | fight off | go into | keep up with | react to | train in |
|---|---|---|---|---|---|

**IN-DEPTH REVIEW** 本文の内容に合うようにa～cから( )に適切な語句を選びましょう。

1

1. The new toothpaste is supposed to do a good job in ( ).
   a. swallowing the ingredients with ease
   b. delivering allergens to immune cells
   c. exposing patients to an excessive amount of an allergen
2. The sublingual treatment is a decent method that ( ).
   a. produces fewer harmful effects
   b. maintains tolerance in every child
   c. triggers no allergic reactions

2

1. One of the problems with sublingual treatment is that the immune cells ( ).
   a. reject routine daily doses of allergens
   b. are abundant on the surface of the cheek
   c. are not dense just under the tongue
2. The clinical trial of the toothpaste will examine ( ).
   a. how effectively the allergen cures patients
   b. whether people can tolerate a large dose of the allergen
   c. to what extent the immunity can be trusted

DL 33　CD2-34

## Summary

**以下の a ~ d を本文に出てきた順番に合うように並べ替え、それぞれの Part の要約文を作りましょう。最後に音声を聞いて確認しましょう。**

Part 1

a. Newly developed toothpaste may be more effective than existing therapies.

b. Putting liquid drops of allergen under the tongue is a milder treatment.

c. If patients are given small bits of peanut protein regularly, it will help maintain tolerance to that allergen.

d. In case of therapy, patients are asked to swallow doses of allergen.

Part 2

a. Sublingual therapy can do a good job, though it is not always easy for patients to continue the treatment.

b. One company started a clinical test of the toothpaste to put the theory into practice.

c. The idea that the allergen can be contained in toothpaste flashed into Bill's mind when he was brushing the teeth.

d. Some allergists favorably look on the idea of toothpaste therapy, but others are worried about the product for safety's sake.

## Writing Strategy

**日本語の意味に合うように [　　] 内の語を並べ替え、英文を完成させましょう。**

1. この治療は、アレルギー反応に対する耐性を作る仕事を上手に行った。
   The new therapy did [ *a* / *at* / *building* / *good job* / *tolerances* ] to allergic reactions.

2. アレルゲンを歯磨き粉に入れて免疫細胞に直に届くようにする、という考えは、一見したところでは、常識外れに思えた。
   The idea of putting an allergen in toothpaste and [ *access* / *direct* / *have* / *it* / *letting* / *to* ] immune cells seemed crazy at first glance.

## Clue to Usage

### do a good job ... の周辺

do a good jobは「上手な仕事をする」。goodの代わりにgreatでもよい。反対にbad [poor]ならけなす表現。do a better job than ... (ℓ. 10) と比較の形もある。仕事の内容を示すのに使われる前置詞は、いろいろある。

ex) The engineer did a good job at fixing the car. / My mother did a great job of raising us kids.

他に do a good job in ～ingもある。また、こうした前置詞を省くスタイルもある。

ex) She did a good job guiding us around the city.

### helpの自由自在

以下の2つの表現 help them to build ... (ℓ. 5)「…を作る手助けをする」と help allergy sufferers keep up with ... (ℓ. 7)「…を維持するのを助ける」はよく似ている。違いはtoの有無だが、helpの後に続くのは不定詞でも原形でもよい。さらに動名詞が続く次のような用法もある。

ex) I cannot help arguing with my brother about nothing.「私はどうでもよいことで弟と言い争うのを止められない」

この文のhelpは用法が本文のものとは違い、avoidやstopの意味を表している。

DL 34　CD2-35

## Approaching the Contents

**質問文の下線部分を書き取り、解答をa～dから選びましょう。**

1 Q: What idea did researchers get as an ______________________ to keep up with regular treatment of food allergies?

a. The new idea was to treat the allergy without causing any side effects.
b. It was such a good idea that the immune cells were protected very effectively.
c. They came up with the idea of putting the allergen in toothpaste.
d. They hit on the idea of putting a food protein just under the tongue.

2 Q: Why are some allergists ______________________ the new treatment?

a. Because the allergen might be able to get into the bloodstream directly, triggering wider allergic reactions.
b. Because it would be difficult for people to maintain the daily treatment.
c. Because it may cause a patient to lose a tooth without his/her knowing it.
d. Because the toothpaste concept has not been approved by the authorities.

# Over to you!

**1～4 はアレルギーに関する FAQ です。質問に対する回答を (a) ～ (d) から選びましょう。また、[　　] に適切な語を Keywords から選び、(a) ～ (d) の英文を完成させましょう。**

**FAQs**

1. What are some common symptoms of food allergies? (　　)
2. What is the mechanism of allergies in general? (　　)
3. How can I distinguish between an allergic response and the symptom of a common cold? (　　)
4. How do I treat allergy symptoms? (　　)

**Answers**

**Keywords** 1. available / 2. harmful / 3. contagious / 4. particular

(a) In both cases, you suffer from similar symptoms, such as sneezing, a runny nose, and headaches. However, itchy eyes are more common with allergies caused by hay fever. Added to that, allergies are not [　　　　], that is, you do not catch them from other people.

(b) Sickness in the stomach, and/or difficulty in breathing, are typical symptoms. Most likely, they start immediately after eating [　　　　] foods, such as peanuts, wheat, eggs, etc. which ordinarily do not have a bad influence on other people.

(c) The immune system in your body reacts to allergen or unfamiliar substances from the outside that are recognized as [　　　　]. Protective antibodies are produced and they start to fight against such allergens, which causes various allergy symptoms.

(d) As prevention is always better than a cure, it is the best policy to avoid any allergy-triggering substances. However, if you have any symptoms, you might as well take medication to relieve them. Your doctor can prescribe the proper ones, and some over-the-counter drugs are also [　　　　].

# Unit 12

## NASA's DART Spacecraft

### 小惑星の衝突から地球を守る

無人探査機による小惑星衝突実験の成功は快挙として報じられました。実験の目的は、衝突時の衝撃で小惑星の軌道を変えることです。今回の対象は地球に無害な小惑星でしたが、衝突回避不能な軌道で進む小惑星がないとも限りません。緻密な計算に基づく大胆な計画の成功は地球防衛のための確かな足掛かりとなりました。

## Word Choice

**日本語の意味に合うようにa～fから適切な語を選びましょう。ただし、選択肢には解答と関係のないものもあります。**

1

| | | |
|---|---|---|
| **1.** | 小惑星帯を通過する | pass through the (　　　　) belt |
| **2.** | 試作品を用いた実験を行う | carry out an (　　　　) with a prototype |
| **3.** | 素晴らしい勝利を手に入れる | achieve a (　　　　) victory |
| **4.** | 未来の天文学者を目指す | aim to be an (　　　　) in the future |
| **5.** | 望遠鏡を月に向ける | turn a (　　　　) toward the moon |

**a.** asteroid　**b.** astronomer　**c.** collision　**d.** experiment　**e.** smashing　**f.** telescope

2

| | | |
|---|---|---|
| **1.** | 委員会の決定を確認する | (　　　　) the decision made by the committee |
| **2.** | 一時所得を手に入れる | get a (　　　　) income |
| **3.** | 有望なコロナワクチンを開発する | develop a (　　　　) vaccine for COVID-19 |
| **4.** | 生存に必要な食べ物を入手する | get some food (　　　　) for survival |
| **5.** | 次号『ネイチャー』誌を楽しみにする | look forward to the (　　　　) issue of *Nature* |

**a.** confirm　**b.** crucial　**c.** length　**d.** promising　**e.** temporary　**f.** upcoming

DL 35 CD2-36 ~ CD2-45

# Reading

## NASA's DART spacecraft successfully bumped an asteroid onto a new path

*Part 1*

It worked! Humans have, for the first time, purposely moved a celestial object.

On September 26, NASA's DART spacecraft rammed into an asteroid named Dimorphos. It struck the space rock at about 22,500 kilometers per hour (nearly 14,000 miles per hour). Its goal? To bump Dimorphos slightly closer to the larger asteroid it orbits, Didymos.

The experiment was a smashing success. Before the impact, Dimorphos orbited Didymos every 11 hours and 55 minutes. After, its orbit was 11 hours and 23 minutes. That 32-minute difference was far greater than astronomers expected. NASA announced these results on October 11 in a news briefing.

Neither Dimorphos nor Didymos poses any threat to Earth. DART's mission was to help scientists find out if a similar impact could nudge an asteroid out of the way if one was ever seen to be on a collision course with Earth.

"For the first time ever, humanity has changed the orbit of a planetary body," said Lori Glaze. She directs NASA's planetary-science division, in Washington, D.C.

Four telescopes in Chile and South Africa watched Dimorphos and Didymos every night after DART's impact. The telescopes can't see the asteroids separately. But they can see the asteroids' combined brightness. That brightness changes as Dimorphos transits (passes in front of) and or passes behind Didymos. The pace of those changes reveals how fast Dimorphos orbits Didymos.

*Part 2*

All four telescopes saw brightness changes consistent with an 11-hour, 23-minute orbit. The result was confirmed by two planetary-radar facilities. Those instruments bounced

*Notes*

- celestial object 天体
- spacecraft 宇宙船
- rammed into ～ ～に突っ込んだ
- orbits 軌道を回る
- news briefing 記者会見
- nudge ～をそっと押して動かす
- collision 衝突
- planetary body 惑星体
- division 部門
- transits 通過する
- planetary-radar facility 惑星レーダー装置
- bounced radio waves off ～ 電波を～に跳ね返らせた

radio waves off the asteroids to measure their orbits directly.

The DART team aimed to change Dimorphos' orbit by at least 73 seconds. The mission overshot that goal by more than 30 minutes. The team thinks the huge plume of debris that the impact kicked up gave the mission extra oomph. DART's impact itself gave the asteroid a push. But the debris flying off in the other direction pushed the space rock even more. The debris plume basically acted like a temporary rocket engine for the asteroid.

overshot ～を超えた
plume of debris 破片の噴出
oomph 力

"This is a very exciting and promising result for planetary defense," said Nancy Chabot. This planetary scientist works at Johns Hopkins Applied Physics Laboratory in Laurel, Md. That's the lab in charge of the DART mission.

The length of Dimorphos' orbit changed by 4 percent. "It just gave it a small nudge," Chabot said. So, knowing an asteroid is coming far ahead of time is crucial for a defense system. For something similar to work on an asteroid headed for Earth, she said, "you'd want to do it years in advance." An upcoming space telescope called Near-Earth Object Surveyor could help provide such an early warning.

gave it a small nudge それを軽く押した
headed for ～ ～に向かった

(442 words)

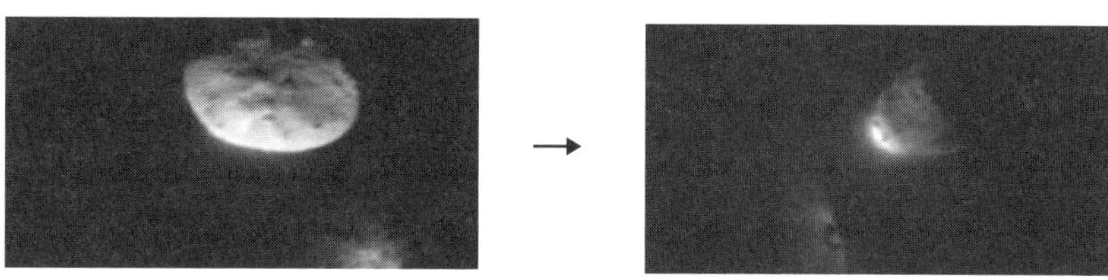

*Further Notes*

ℓ.42 **Johns Hopkins Applied Physics Laboratory** ジョンズ・ホプキンス大学応用物理研究所。1942年に設立され、1954年に現在のメリーランド州ローレルに移転した。ジョンズ・ホプキンス大学と提携関係にある非営利の大学付属研究センター。近年、成果を上げている探査機の開発を筆頭に、宇宙分野での科学の発展に大きく貢献している。

ℓ.49 **Near-Earth Object Surveyor** 地球に接近する小惑星の探索を目的に、打ち上げが予定されている宇宙望遠鏡。

## Exercises

KEY PHRASES

（　　）に適切な語句を語群から選び英文を完成させましょう。ただし、必要に応じて語形は変えること。

1. The driver of the car that (　　　　　　　　) the supermarket was reported to be drunk.
2. The new computer virus (　　　　　　　　) to all PC users.
3. The increasing number of typhoons is (　　　　　　　　) recent trends in the weather.
4. The third-year students (　　　　　　　　) taking care of the newcomers in our club.
5. We need to book a restaurant (　　　　　　　　).

| be in charge of | consistent with | in advance | pose a threat | ram into |
|---|---|---|---|---|

IN-DEPTH REVIEW

本文の内容に合うようにa～cから（　　）に適切な語句を選びましょう。

Part 1

1. The 32-minute difference proved that (　　　　).
   a. the orbit of Didymos was successfully altered
   b. NASA achieved great results
   c. the speed of DART was insufficient
2. The impact of the mission was checked by (　　　　).
   a. measuring the timing when Didymos passes behind Dimorphos
   b. using four telescopes mounted on DART
   c. observing the change in asteroids' combined brightness

Part 2

1. NASA thinks that (　　　　) contributed to the greater success of the mission.
   a. the debris produced by the impact
   b. two space-based facilities
   c. measuring the space rocks
2. Nancy Chabot (　　　　).
   a. used Near-Earth Object Surveyor to defend the Earth
   b. appreciates the results of the DART mission
   c. is skeptical about the danger of asteroids

DL 36 CD2-46

## Summary

**以下の a ～ d を本文に出てきた順番に合うように並べ替え、それぞれの Part の要約文を作りましょう。最後に音声を聞いて確認しましょう。**

t 1

[ ] → [ ] → [ ] → [ ]

a. The experiment's result will help scientists cope with an asteroid that poses a threat to Earth.

b. When the two asteroids crossed each other, there was a change in the fluctuations of their combined brightness, which showed how much Dimorphos' orbit had changed.

c. NASA sent the DART spacecraft to bring the asteroid Dimorphos a little closer to another asteroid it orbits.

d. After the impact, Dimorphos' orbital period was shortened by around half an hour.

t 2

[ ] → [ ] → [ ] → [ ]

a. The DART team decided that the debris plume flying off from the asteroid worked like a kind of rocket engine.

b. Dimorphos' orbit had changed far more than expected as the result of an additional push by the debris plume.

c. Knowing well in advance that an asteroid is approaching Earth is very important for planetary defense.

d. The observation results from the telescopes were confirmed by radar facilities.

## Writing Strategy

**日本語の意味に合うように [ ] 内の語を並べ替え、英文を完成させましょう。**

1. 天体から跳ね返される電磁波を分析することで、研究者たちはそれらの天体の動きについて、ずっと詳しい情報を得ることができた。

By analyzing radio waves bounced off the celestial bodies, researchers [ *accurate* / *far* / *information* / *managed* / *more* / *obtain* / *to* ] about their movements.

______________________________

2. 締め切りに遅れないように、十分早めに書類を用意しておくべきですよ。

You [ *ahead* / *documents* / *far* / *of* / *prepare* / *the* / *time* / *to* / *want* ] so that you do not miss the deadline.

______________________________

## Clue to Usage

### wantの使い道

動詞 want の意味は「望む／欲する」で何の問題もなさそうだが、こんな例文はどうだろう。

ex) May I give you a piece of advice? You want to see the doctor now, before it is too late.

助言しているのだから「医者に診てもらうのがよい／診てもらうべきだ」と訳したくなる。wantは語源的には「欠けている／不足している」のような lacking, missingの意味であるため、それを補う「必要がある」needの意味を持つ。例文はneed to seeあるいはshould seeと読み替えればよい。本文の例を挙げると、you'd want to do it years in advance (ℓ. 48)がある。

### 比較級を強める

difference was far greater than ... (ℓ. 11) の副詞 far は「さらに、いっそう」と比較級greaterの程度を強めている。far以外では、muchがポピュラーだが、ほかにもevenやstillがある。

ex) Tomorrow will be even colder because of a cold air mass. / The number of victims is likely to rise still higher.

反対に、「少し」の程度であれば、a little more rainとかslightly closer to ... (ℓ. 6)といった表現になる。その程度を詳しく示すのに数字を使ってfive feet longer than ... / 30 minutes earlier than ... などとすることもできる。さらに、これを少し変えてlonger than ... by five feetなどとby ～の副詞句を入れる形もある。「～の分だけ」を意味するby ～の表現は、by 4 percent (ℓ. 44)など、Part 2に3回出てくる。

## Approaching the Contents

**質問文の下線部分を書き取り、解答をa～dから選びましょう。**

Part 1

**Q:** Does either Dimorphos or Didymos ________________________?

a. If they bumped against each other, it might cause huge damage to Earth.
b. Nobody knows exactly what will happen after an asteroid collides with Earth.
c. Neither of the asteroids is likely to do harm to Earth.
d. As asteroids should break into pieces, they are no menace to Earth.

Part 2

**Q:** What did the scientist team ________________________ DART ram into an asteroid?

a. Scientists tried to issue an early warning about a shooting star.
b. Their initial goal was to give the asteroid just a small push.
c. They planned to do experiments on a rocket engine near an asteroid.
d. They intended to demonstrate how effectively the planetary radar works.

# Over to you!

**1～3 は NASA's DART mission について書かれた文章です。[　　] に入る適切な語を Keywords から選びましょう。また、提示されている英文が正しい場合は T、誤っている場合は F で答えましょう。**

**Keywords** collision / debris / eclipse / origin

**1.** Billions of small rocky objects called asteroids gather around in the main asteroid belt, between Mars and Jupiter. They are of various shapes and sizes. Small bits of asteroids may sometimes fly through the Earth's atmosphere as shooting stars and, if they don't burn out during the journey, they may land on the surface. They are called meteorites. *Hayabusa* missions from Japan returned some samples of asteroids, which may endow scientists with clues about the [　　　　] of the planets and life.

[T / F] A great number of rocky objects called asteroids are scattered across the space between the orbits of the two planets Jupiter and Mars.

[T / F] By analyzing samples from asteroids, scientists may obtain useful information about how the planets and life began.

**2.** Astronomical transits are noticed when a celestial body passes between a larger body (the Sun, for example) and us, the observer on Earth. One typical case is a solar [　　　　] by the Moon. Venus and Mercury that orbit inside the Earth give us similar scenes of transit when they move in front of the Sun. NASA's Kepler space telescope has discovered extra-solar planets using technology to detect astronomical transits.

[T / F] As long as we stay on Earth, we can't see Mars or Jupiter transiting the Sun.

[T / F] If you could land on Mars in the future, you may have the opportunity to witness the Earth transiting the Sun.

**3.** Will a super-sized asteroid ever hit the Earth? Many of the meteorites will burn up while falling through the atmosphere. Still, a huge asteroid may be on a [　　　　] course. If such an asteroid were to hit the Earth, it may cause the extinction of the human race. The best policy is to find such menaces as early as possible in order to give an advance warning.

[T / F] A huge asteroid that wipes out humans may appear soon.

[T / F] New technology will launch the Earth into a new orbit to evade a collision.

# Unit 13

# What Is Sickle Cell Disease?

## 鎌状赤血球症を知っていますか？

鎌状赤血球症は、赤血球の形状が鎌状に変化すると共に体内に酸素を運ぶ機能の低下を伴う血液の病気です。アフリカに患者が多数みられ、マラリアとの係りが指摘されています。難治性疾患のひとつという従来の位置づけが、科学の進歩によって変わる可能性が見えてきました。

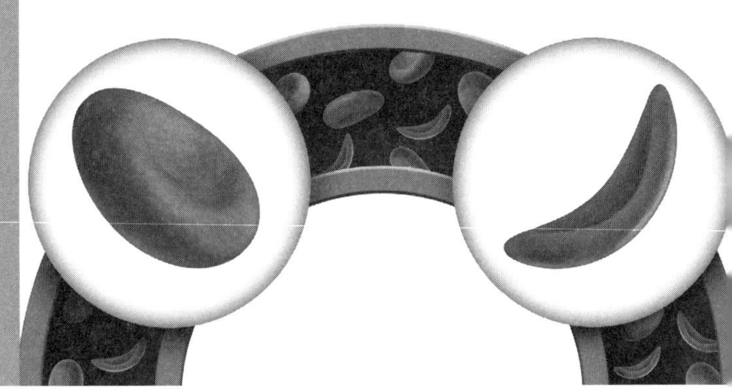

## Word Choice

**日本語の意味に合うように a ～ f から適切な語を選びましょう。ただし、選択肢には解答と関係のないものもあります。**

Part 1

| | | |
|---|---|---|
| 1. | 分子レベルの誤差を検出する | detect errors at the (　　　　) level |
| 2. | 重症患者を病院へ運ぶ | (　　　　) a critically ill patient to a hospital |
| 3. | 紙を三日月形に切る | cut paper in a (　　　　) shape |
| 4. | 柔軟性のない規則を改定する | revise the (　　　　) rules |
| 5. | 彼の成功談を文字通り受け取る | take his success story (　　　　) |

a. crescent　b. inflexible　c. literally　d. molecular　e. transport　f. underlie

Part 2

| | | |
|---|---|---|
| 1. | 前首相の権力を受け継ぐ | (　　　　) the authority of the former prime minister |
| 2. | 新製品の予想売上高を報告する | report the (　　　　) sales of the new product |
| 3. | 職場内ストレスへの抵抗力をつける | build up a (　　　　) to stress in the office |
| 4. | 舞台裏から現れる | (　　　　) from backstage |
| 5. | 心臓移植のドナーを探す | look for a donor for a heart (　　　　) |

a. afflict　b. emerge　c. estimated　d. inherit　e. resistance　f. transplant

# Reading

## What is sickle cell disease?

*Part 1*

Notes

Our genes serve as an operating manual for the cells of the body. Genes tell cells what to do and when. But copying errors in those operating manuals — known as mutations— can lead to misspelled instructions that can change how cells operate. Scientists now know that some of those mutations can lead to disease. Others offer benefits. Some can do both. And the mutation that underlies sickle cell disease is one that can be both good and very bad.

mutation 突然変異

underlies 根底にある
sickle cell disease 鎌状赤血球症

Sickle cell disease is caused by a molecular change in the body's hemoglobin.

Hemoglobin is the molecule in red blood cells that transports oxygen to tissues throughout the body. It wasn't until 1949 that scientists learned that altered hemoglobin causes red blood cells to take the shape of crescent moons. In fact, this condition was the first known example of a disease linked to inherited changes in a molecule.

Hemoglobin normally allows "red blood cells to be very floppy and pliable, and slip and slide through the blood vessels easily," says Erica Esrick. She's a pediatrician at Boston Children's Hospital and Harvard Medical School. Both are in Boston, Mass.

floppy and pliable 柔らかくしなやか
pediatrician 小児科医

Boston, Mass. マサチューセッツ州ボストン

But a mutation in a single hemoglobin-making gene — the *HBB* gene — underlies sickle cell disease. This mutation makes hemoglobin stack in long strings inside blood cells. It gives those cells an inflexible, sickle — or crescent-moon — shape. Instead of being "squishy," the now-stiff red blood cells get stuck inside blood vessels. This can cause severe and debilitating pain. Worse still, the sickle cells can literally block blood flow and the movement of oxygen into nearby tissues.

squishy ぐにゃぐにゃする

get stuck 詰まる

debilitating 消耗性の

*Part 2*

Most people with sickle cell disease live only into their late 40s. Among other reasons, the blocked blood vessels that this disease often causes can lead to strokes or organ damage.

To develop this disease, people must inherit that mutant *HBB* gene from both parents. If they get the mutant from one parent only, their blood cells can work normally.

Sickle cell affects millions of people around the world. In the United States, for instance, about 100,000 people live with the disease. Most of them are Black or Latino. The mutation behind it is particularly common in people whose ancestors came from parts of Africa that are south of the Sahara, from parts of the Middle East, or Southeast Asia. Why?

It turns out that these areas have high rates of malaria.

Malaria afflicts an estimated 241 million people. In 2020 alone, it killed an estimated 627,000 people, according to the World Health Organization. And the mutant *HBB* gene makes the body resistant to infection by the parasite that causes malaria. Once the mutant gene first emerged, it spread widely in parts of the world where it conferred this resistance to malaria. But that benefit is overshadowed when someone inherits the mutant gene from both parents and develops sickle cell disease.

A bone marrow transplant is currently the only cure for sickle cell disease. A new marrow can make un-sickled red blood cells. But such transplants are costly. Finding a matched donor to contribute marrow also is challenging, Esrick notes. That's one reason researchers have begun looking to replace the mutant *HBB* genes. Esrick is part of one research team that is currently trying to fight the disease through gene therapy.

(544 words)

stroke 脳卒中

mutant 突然変異による。なお、次行のmutantは突然変異体（名詞）。

Black or Latino 黒人かラテン系の人々

parasite 寄生虫

conferred 与えた

is overshadowed （恩恵が）弱まる

bone marrow 骨髄

challenging 難しい

*Further Notes*

ℓ.20 **Harvard Medical School**　ハーバード大学医学大学院。1782 年に設立されたハーバード大学の専門職大学院の１つ。マサチューセッツ州ボストンにある。日本で言う医学部のようなところで、医師を養成する学校である。

ℓ.22 ***HBB* gene**　ヘモグロビンサブユニットベータ遺伝子。ヘモグロビン (Hb) を構成するタンパク質（サブユニット）の１つである β (beta) - グロビンの設計図となる遺伝子で、鎌状赤血球症の原因遺伝子にあたる。

ℓ.41 **malaria**　熱帯、亜熱帯地方に広く分布する感染症。マラリア原虫をもった蚊に刺されることで感染する。世界三大感染症（マラリア、結核、HIV/AIDS ）の１つ。

## Exercises

**KEY PHRASES**

**(　　) に適切な語句を語群から選び英文を完成させましょう。ただし、必要に応じて語形は変えること。**

1. She is willing to (　　　　　　　　　) a volunteer worker at the conference.
2. He (　　　　　　　　　) an expert in tropical diseases now.
3. In some cases, headaches (　　　　　　　　　) a lack of sleep.
4. The suitcase (　　　　　　　　　) in the x-ray machine because it was too big.
5. It's hard to (　　　　　　　　　) chronic pain in the back.

| be caused by | be known as | get stuck | live with | serve as |
|---|---|---|---|---|

**IN-DEPTH REVIEW**

**本文の内容に合うようにa～cから(　　)に適切な語句を選びましょう。**

t 1

1. The genes of our body (　　　　).
   a. are closely linked to sickle cell disease
   b. act as operating manuals to tell cells how to function
   c. protect us from misspelled instructions that can lead to disease
2. The mutation in a hemoglobin-making gene (　　　　).
   a. can send wrong messages to a disease
   b. can bring about benefits to the health
   c. can cause trouble in red blood cells

t 2

1. Thanks to the mutant *HBB* gene, people are able to (　　　　).
   a. acquire resistance to malaria
   b. be afflicted by the parasite
   c. live with the disease for a while
2. The only medical treatment for sickle cell disease is (　　　　).
   a. a bone marrow transplant
   b. a fight through gene therapy
   c. a mutant gene from both parents

DL 39 CD2-59

## Summary

**以下の a ～ d を本文に出てきた順番に合うように並べ替え、それぞれの Part の要約文を作りましょう。最後に音声を聞いて確認しましょう。**

Part 1

□ → □ → □ → □

a. Sickle cell disease will force acute pain on the patient.

b. Any errors that happen in our genes could send incorrect information to cells.

c. If a molecular change in a body's hemoglobin occurs, red blood cells would develop into sickle forms.

d. When it is in normal condition, hemoglobin allows red blood cells to move smoothly in blood vessels.

Part 2

a. The mutation in a hemoglobin-making gene is common in Black or Latino people in particular.

b. Sickle cell disease can be treated by a bone marrow transplant, though it is very expensive.

c. Sickle cell disease can trigger organ disorders and strokes.

d. People will be endowed with resistance to malaria with the help of the mutant *HBB* gene.

## Writing Strategy

**日本語の意味に合うように [　　] 内の語を並べ替え、英文を完成させましょう。**

1. 最近になって初めて、ウエブ上で操作マニュアルが参照できるようになった。
   [ *could* / *not* / *recently* / *refer* / *to* / *until* / *you* ] an operating manual on the Web.

   ______________________________

2. 推定で何百万という人々が、この病気に冒されていることが分かった。
   [ *an* / *estimated* / *it* / *millions* / *of* / *out* / *that* / *turned* ] people are affected by the disease.

   ______________________________

## Clue to Usage

### worseのレシピ

Part 1の末尾で、badやillの比較級worseが副詞句worse stillの形で使われており、「いっそう悪いことには」と訳せる。似た表現としては、以下の例文のようなものがある。

ex) It was after dark when my car broke down, and to make matters worse, it started to rain.

この文にあるto make matters worse, の部分は関係代名詞を使い、what is worse とも表現できる。この２つをより簡略にしたのが本文にあるworse stillだ。

### untilの収まり具合

It wasn't until 1949 that scientists learned that altered hemoglobin causes red blood cells to take the shape of crescent moons. (ℓ. 12) は「1949年になって初めて、変異ヘモグロビンが赤血球を三日月形にすることを科学者たちは知った」と意味を取ることができる。この文は、長いため簡単な例文で考えてみよう。

ex) You cannot go outside until you finish the meal.「食事がすむまでは、外へ出てはいけない」

①否定の意味合いを強める場合

Notと共に副詞節(句)をまとめて文頭に出す。

Not until you finish the meal, can you go outside.

②文意をより強める場合

本文に登場する It is ... that...の強調構文を使って、以下のようにも表現できる。

It is not until you finish the meal that you can go outside.

訳す際には「～して初めて」と意味を取る。

## Approaching the Contents

**質問文の下線部分を書き取り、解答をａ～ｄから選びましょう。**

**Q:** What happens when hemoglobin has ______________________?

a. Hemoglobin is given a sickle-like form.
b. Altered hemoglobin will finally take a crescent-moon shape.
c. Blood vessels, as well as nearby tissues, become inflexible.
d. Blood flow is blocked and the supply of oxygen is decreased.

**Q:** What is the necessary condition for people to ______________________?

a. They must inherit a specific mutant gene from both parents.
b. Oxygen-carrying blood cells must be blocked.
c. First of all, it is necessary to fight the disease by gene therapy.
d. Malaria is responsible for the onset of the disease.

# Over to you!

**1～4は血液に関するFAQです。質問に対する回答を (a) ～ (d) から選びましょう。また、[　　]に適切な語をKeywordsから選び、(a) ～ (d) の英文を完成させましょう。**

**FAQs**

1. Where are the blood cells made? (　　)
2. What gives blood its color? (　　)
3. How much blood is in the human body? (　　)
4. What are the components of blood? (　　)

**Answers**

**Keywords** 1. inside / 2. factors / 3. make up / 4. transports

(a) They are made in the bone marrow. It is the soft, spongy tissue [　　　] of the bones in our body. It produces about 95% of the body's blood cells.

(b) The blood components are red blood cells, white blood cells, plasma*, and platelets**. Red blood cells comprise about 44%, white blood cells and platelets [　　　] about 1%, and plasma constitutes 55% of total blood volume.

(c) It's hemoglobin in red blood cells. Hemoglobin [　　　] oxygen through our body. Each hemoglobin molecule includes a protein called hem that contains iron. When iron reacts with oxygen, it becomes red.

(d) There is an estimated 5 liters of blood in the average adult human body, but this number will vary depending on [　　　] such as age, size, and where they live. For example, people who live at high altitudes have more blood because there is less oxygen at high altitudes.

*plasma「血しょう」 **platelete「血小板」

# Unit 14 The Doppler Effect

## 広がる応用、ドップラー効果

救急車のサイレンや踏切の警報音といった身近な例で説明されるドップラー効果。比較的単純な原理に基づくこの現象は、さまざまな分野における応用を可能にしています。たとえば、身体に負担をかけずに非接触で体内の状況を確認できる超音波センサーや血流測定器は、ドップラー効果の特徴を活かして開発された医療機器です。

## Word Choice

**日本語の意味に合うように a ～ f から適切な語を選びましょう。ただし、選択肢には解答と関係のないものもあります。**

1

| | |
|---|---|
| 1. 中立的な観察者の役割を果たす | play a role as a neutral (　　　　) |
| 2. 彼女の声のかすかな変化に気付く | (　　　　) a slight change in her voice |
| 3. 超音波を発する | (　　　　) ultrasound waves |
| 4. 最悪のシナリオを想像したくない | hate to (　　　　) the worst scenario |
| 5. 盗聴を恐れて周波数を変える | scramble the (　　　　) for fear of eavesdropping |

**a.** emit　**b.** frequency　**c.** idle　**d.** observer　**e.** perceive　**f.** picture

2

| | |
|---|---|
| 1. 近代天文学の誕生をたどる | trace the birth of modern (　　　　) |
| 2. 波長が合っている | be on the same (　　　　) |
| 3. 巨大銀河から得たデータを分析する | analyze the data taken from a massive (　　　　) |
| 4. 車両の際立った安定性を宣伝する | advertise the outstanding (　　　　) stability |
| 5. 配送状況を追跡する | (　　　　) the status of the shipment |

**a.** astronomy　**b.** galaxy　**c.** track　**d.** vehicle　**e.** wavelength　**f.** wobble

## Reading

### Doppler effect

*Part 1*

Notes

The Doppler effect is a change in the apparent wavelength of light or sound waves. This change is caused by the source of those waves moving toward or away from an observer. If a wave source moves toward an observer, then that observer perceives shorter waves than the source actually emitted. If a wave source moves away from an observer, then that observer perceives longer waves than those actually emitted.

To picture why this happens, imagine that you are driving a motorboat in the ocean. Waves roll toward the shore at a constant rate. And if your boat sits idle on the water, waves will pass you at that constant rate. But if you drive your boat out to sea — toward the wave source — then waves will pass your boat at a higher frequency. In other words, the waves' wavelength will seem shorter from your point of view. Now, imagine driving your boat back to shore. In this case, you are moving away from the source of the waves. Each wave passes your boat at a slower rate. That is, the waves' wavelength seems longer from your perspective. No matter which way you drive your boat, the ocean waves themselves have not changed. Only your experience of them has. The same is true with the Doppler effect.

roll toward the shore 岸へ打ち寄せる

point of view 視点

perspective 視点

You may have heard the Doppler effect at work in the sound of a siren. As a siren approaches you, you perceive its sound waves as shorter. Shorter sound waves have a higher pitch. Then, when the siren passes you and gets farther away, its sound waves seem longer. Those longer sound waves have a lower frequency and pitch.

pitch 音の高さ

*Part 2*

The Doppler effect plays an important role in astronomy. That's because stars and other celestial objects give off light waves. When a celestial object moves toward Earth, its light

celestial object 天体

waves appear bunched up. These shorter light waves look bluer. This phenomenon is called blueshift. When an object moves away from Earth, its light waves seem stretched out. Longer light waves look redder, so this effect is called redshift. Blueshift and redshift can expose slight wobbles in stars' motions. Those wobbles help astronomers detect the gravitational pull of planets. The redshift of distant galaxies also helped reveal that the universe is expanding.

Some technology relies on the Doppler effect. To catch people who are speeding, police officers point radar devices at cars. Those machines send out radio waves, which bounce off moving vehicles. Because of the Doppler effect, the waves reflected by moving cars have a different wavelength than those sent out by the radar device. That difference shows how fast a car is moving.

Meteorologists use similar tech to send radio waves into the atmosphere. Changes in the wavelengths of waves reflected back allow scientists to track water in the atmosphere. This helps them forecast the weather.

The Doppler effect helped one teen discover a planet with two suns, like Luke Skywalker's home planet in *Star Wars*.

(493 words)

bunched up 束になった
blueshift 青方偏移
stretched out 引き伸ばされた
redshift 赤方偏移
wobble 揺れ
gravitational pull 引力
bounce off ～ ～に当たって跳ね返る
meteorologists 気象学者

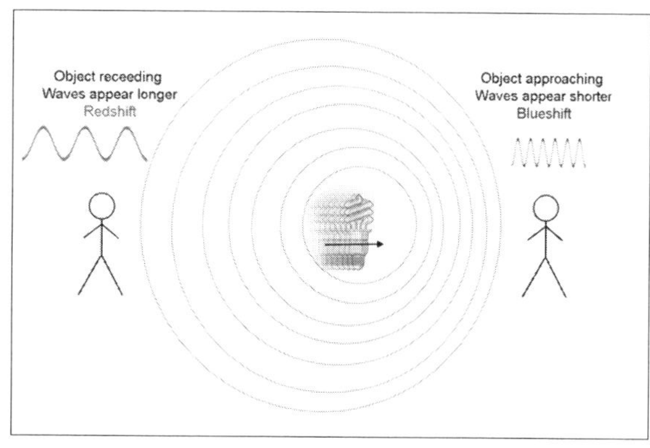


## *Further Notes*

ℓ.51 **Luke Skywalker's home planet in *Star Wars*** 映画『スター・ウォーズ』(1977年に公開されたアメリカのシリーズもの SF 映画) の登場人物ルーク・スカイウォーカーの故郷にあたる砂漠の惑星タトゥイーン (Tatooine) を指す。2つの太陽 (連星) を周回している。

## Exercises

KEY PHRASES　(　　)に適切な語句を語群から選び英文を完成させましょう。ただし、必要に応じて語形は変えること。

1. To avoid becoming infected with COVID-19, I always (　　　　　　　　) crowds.
2. They found the airplane crash site because the radio was (　　　　　　　　) a weak signal.
3. Exhausted after the long journey, I felt like (　　　　　　　　) on a bed.
4. The player caught the ball nicely as it (　　　　　　　　) the wall.
5. The politician makes it a rule to (　　　　　　　　) a message on Twitter every morning.

| bounce off | give off | move away from | send out | stretch out |
|---|---|---|---|---|

IN-DEPTH REVIEW　本文の内容に合うようにa～cから(　　)に適切な語句を選びましょう。

Part 1

1. When a wave source moves away from you, you perceive (　　　　).
   a. the shorter waves that pass you at a constant rate
   b. that the wavelength of the waves is longer than it actually is
   c. an apparent wavelength of light
2. If you drive your boat out to sea at a certain speed, (　　　　).
   a. the length between the waves will seem to get longer
   b. the actual frequency of the ocean waves tends to be lower
   c. the ocean waves seem to pass you at a higher frequency

Part 2

1. The wavelengths of radio waves that bounce off of a passing vehicle are (　　　　).
   a. quite similar to the signals directed by the police radar
   b. not the same as recorded on the vehicle onboard device
   c. different from those first transmitted from the radar device
2. Using radio waves reflected from the atmosphere, meteorologists can (　　　　).
   a. detect slight wobbles of stars
   b. track moisture in the air
   c. discover an extra-solar planet

DL 42 CD2-68

## Summary

**以下の a ～ d を本文に出てきた順番に合うように並べ替え、それぞれの Part の要約文を作りましょう。最後に音声を聞いて確認しましょう。**

rt 1

a. If the boat that carries you is moving toward the shore, each wavelength appears to be stretching longer from your viewpoint.

b. The Doppler effect may be clearly illustrated if you imagine you are driving a boat on the sea.

c. The wavelengths of sound and light change depending on whether their source is approaching you or not.

d. A common experience of the Doppler effect is the sound of a siren, where you hear a higher pitch, and then a lower pitch, as the source of the sound passes.

rt 2

☐ → ☐ → ☐ → ☐

a. The Doppler effect is applied not only to sound waves but to light waves, too.

b. If you send radio waves into the atmosphere, and detect changes in reflected waves, the data can be used to forecast the weather.

c. Using the radio waves reflected by a moving vehicle enables you to estimate its speed.

d. Astronomers assumed that small wobbles of the stars are caused by planets orbiting them.

## Writing Strategy

**日本語の意味に合うように [　　] 内の語 (句) を並べ替え、英文を完成させましょう。**

1. 我々は、実際に発せられたものよりも、見かけ上、より高い周波数の音波を聞いている。
We perceive the sound waves that apparently have [ *a* / *emitted* / *frequency* / *higher* / *actually* / *than* / *those* ].

______________________________________________

2. 恒星の動きの中に生じたわずかの揺れを観察することができるならば、その場合は、この現象が、天文学者たちに惑星の引力の検知を可能にさせるだろう。
If astronomers were able to observe slight wobbles in the motion of the stars, [ *allow them* / *could* / *detect* / *the phenomenon* / *then* / *to* ] the gravitational pull of planets.

______________________________________________

## Clue to Usage

### If ～ then ... の構文

副詞 thenは、in that caseという表現と同じように、先行する内容を受けて「それなら／その場合は」という意味で使える。If a wave source moves toward an observer, then that observer perceives ... (ℓ. 3)「音源が聴いているその人にもし近づいてくるならば、するとその場合は…」という意味になる。

### apparentから見えるもの

apparent wavelength of light or sound waves (ℓ. 1)「光ないし音波のapparent な波長」という意味に取れる。形容詞apparentには以下のように、やや異質な２つの意味と使い方がある。

①「明らかな」(類語：obvious, evident)

ex) The truth has now become apparent to the jury.「陪審員たちとって真実は明らかになった」

②「見かけ上の」(類語：seeming to be true)

ex) Don't trust his apparent friendliness. He's a liar.「彼の見せかけの友情を信じてはいけない」

このユニットの場合、actually (ℓ. 5)「実際に／本当に」を参考にして、②の用例が使われていると考える。

なお、派生語の副詞apparentlyは②の延長線上の「見かけ上では」の意味で使う例が多い。

ex) I'm not certain about it, but apparently, they got divorced.

「明らかに」と言いたいときは、誤解のないようobviouslyやevidentlyを使うのが良い。

DL 43 CD2-69

## Approaching the Contents

**質問文の下線部分を書き取り、解答をａ～ｄから選びましょう。**

Part 1

Q: ________________________________, is there any difference between the workings of ocean waves and the sound waves of a siren?

a. Ocean waves repeat some regular movements, which you cannot expect from sound waves.

b. Their effects are quite similar to each other, only ocean waves resemble light waves more closely.

c. Both waves work on the same physical principle and produce similar effects.

d. Unlike ocean waves, the sound waves of a siren do not reach you at a constant rate.

Part 2

Q: How are astronomers able to conclude that ________________________?

a. By detecting the phenomenon called blueshift.

b. By irregular wobbles in the motion of the stars.

c. By observations of light waves that look redder than before.

d. By noticing light waves that appear bunched together.

# Over to you!

**1 ～ 3 は Doppler の生涯について書かれた文章です。[　　] に入る適切な語を Keywords から選びましょう。また、提示されている英文が正しい場合は T、誤っている場合は F で答えましょう。**

**Keywords**　brilliant / graduated / position / tried

**1.** Christian Doppler was born on 29 November, 1803 in Austria, the son of a renowned stonemason. Because of his poor health, he could not work in his father's business. To get professional training in commerce, he attended three years of middle school in Salzburg and an additional fourth year in Linz. After the completion of his studies in Linz, he was sent to the Polytechnic Institute. He [　　　　] with excellent grades in 1825 in Vienna.

[T / F] Doppler was not physically strong enough to take over his father's business.

[T / F] At the age of 22, Doppler stayed in Linz for seven years to attend middle school.

**2.** After his education at the Polytechnic, Doppler completed the Gymnasium and subsequent courses in an amazingly short time. Then he returned to Vienna and was employed as an assistant for higher mathematics at the Polytechnic Institute. In 1835, he got a [　　　　] as a professor of accounting and mathematics at the State Secondary School in Prague. The next year, Doppler got married. The Doppler family lived in Prague and was blessed with five children.

[T / F] Doppler was employed as a professor at the Polytechnic Institute.

[T / F] Mr. and Mrs. Doppler started their life together in Prague in 1836.

**3.** In 1841, Doppler became a professor at the State Technical Academy in Prague. One year later, he published his most [　　　　] work on the Doppler effect. As a result of the Hungarian Revolution in 1848, the Doppler family fled to Vienna, where he was appointed head of the Institute of experimental physics at the University of Vienna in 1850. In 1852, he made a trip to Venice in the hope of recovering his ill health, but it was in vain. He died there the following year, survived by his family.

[T / F] The Doppler family protested strongly against the Hungarian Revolution in 1841.

[T / F] Coming back to Prague, Doppler died in his hometown when he was 51.

# Unit 15

# Surviving a Trip to Mars

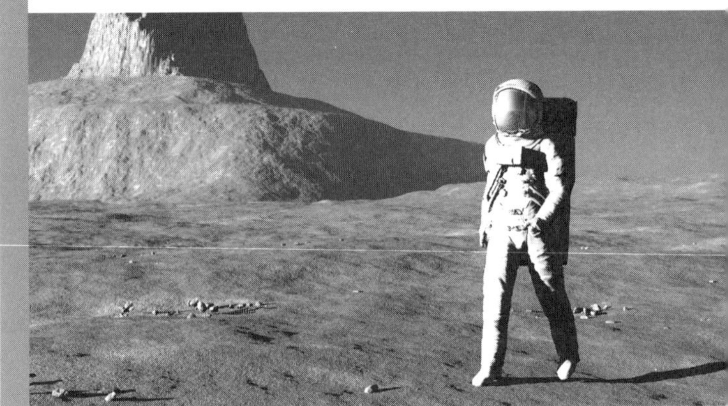

## 困難を乗り越え 火星へ

人類最大のチャレンジとも言われる火星への有人飛行。宇宙工学、宇宙生物学、宇宙医学など、科学の諸領域が融合し、最先端のテクノロジーを武器に総力を挙げて困難に立ち向かっています。2020 年に打ち上げられた探査機 Perseverance の意味は「不屈の努力」。困難にひるまない人類の努力が実を結ぶ日は遠くはないかもしれません。

## Word Choice

**日本語の意味に合うように a ～ f から適切な語を選びましょう。ただし、選択肢には解答と関係のないものもあります。**

### Part 1

| | | |
|---|---|---|
| 1. | 社説で政治の領域を扱う | cover the (　　　　) of politics in the editorial |
| 2. | 科学の世界で画期的なことを達成する | achieve a (　　　　) in science |
| 3. | 有名な宇宙飛行士を講演に招く | invite a famous (　　　　) to the lecture |
| 4. | 放射線被ばくを防ぐ | prevent (　　　　) exposure |
| 5. | 宇宙の旅を思い描く | dream up a (　　　　) journey |

**a.** astronaut　**b.** cosmic　**c.** domain　**d.** explorer　**e.** milestone　**f.** radiation

### Part 2

| | | |
|---|---|---|
| 1. | アレルギーを起こす材料を避ける | avoid allergy-causing (　　　　). |
| 2. | 別の分子と衝突する | collide with another (　　　　) |
| 3. | 不用意な発言で名声を危うくする | (　　　　) your reputation by making careless remarks |
| 4. | コンピュータをウイルスに感染させる | (　　　　) a computer with a virus |
| 5. | 細菌兵器を廃絶する | eliminate a (　　　　) weapon |

**a.** carbon　**b.** compromise　**c.** germ　**d.** infect　**e.** ingredient　**f.** molecule

## Reading

### *Let's learn about surviving a trip to Mars*

*Part 1*

Notes

So far, Mars has been the domain of space robots. Over the last 60 years, many spacecraft have flown by, orbited, and even landed on the Red Planet. But human explorers could work faster and be more flexible than machines. Not to mention, setting foot on Mars would be a major milestone in space exploration. That's why the United States, China, and other countries want to send people to Mars. But surviving this adventure would be no easy feat.

have flown by 近くを飛行した

setting foot on Mars 火星に降り立つこと

A Mars mission would be the farthest journey in human history. At an average of 225 million kilometers (140 million miles) away, Mars would take at least six months for astronauts to reach. (It would take at least another six months to get back home). In contrast, Apollo astronauts got to the moon in a few days.

mission 宇宙飛行

While space travel is never free of danger, the length of a roundtrip to Mars poses many extra health risks. For one thing, floating in microgravity for long periods weakens bones and muscles. Plus, it allows fluid to build up in the head, putting pressure behind the eyes and causing vision problems. Artificial gravity machines could help.

roundtrip 往復旅行

microgravity 微小重力

But then there's space radiation to worry about. The Earth's magnetic field protects astronauts near Earth from high-energy cosmic rays. Those charged particles might raise the risk of cancer and other health problems. On longer journeys, though, astronauts would be exposed for months. Taking certain vitamins could reduce the impact. But scientists are still working out the details.

space radiation 宇宙放射線

charged particle 荷電粒子

*Part 2*

Mars explorers will have to pack light to lift off from Earth. But they won't be able to restock on supplies like astronauts on the space station do. Astronauts on the space station practice

restock 補充する

for this by growing lettuce and other food in space. Engineers are also developing 3-D printing techniques that could let future Mars astronauts build tools as needed. The material for those tools could come from the astronauts themselves. For instance, astronaut pee could feed the yeast that churns out ingredients to make plastic.

- yeast 酵母、イースト
- churns out～ ～を大量生産する

Setting up and surviving at a Mars colony would be even more complicated. Since astronauts can't haul construction materials from Earth, scientists are dreaming up ways for astronauts to use materials on Mars. Long-term visitors would also need plenty of oxygen to breathe. A device on NASA's Perseverance rover is currently laying the groundwork for a future Mars oxygen factory. The device pries oxygen off molecules of carbon dioxide, the main gas in Mars' atmosphere.

- haul ～を運ぶ
- dreaming up ～ ～を思い描く
- is ... laying the groundwork 下準備をしている
- pries oxygen off ～ ～から酸素を引きはがす

Planning for a trip to Mars isn't just about protecting astronauts. It's also about protecting Mars *from* astronauts. Humans are teeming with microbes. And spreading those microbes could compromise the search for life on Mars. As a result, a key part of responsible space exploration is making sure Earth's germs don't infect other planets.

- are teeming with ～ ～で満ち溢れる
- compromise（評判・名声などを）危うくする

(426 words)

*Further Notes*

ℓ.41 **NASA's Perseverance rover** NASA の火星探査計画の一環として 2020 年 7 月に打ち上げられた火星探査機。翌年 2 月に火星に着陸したことが確認された。名前のパーサヴィアランス（Perseverance）は「忍耐」「不屈の努力」という意味。

## Exercises

KEY PHRASES

(　　)に適切な語句を語群から選び英文を完成させましょう。ただし、必要に応じて語形は変えること。

1. The patient had an operation to get rid of the fluid (　　　　　　　　) his lungs.
2. The TV scriptwriter tried hard to (　　　　　　　　) the plot of the new drama.
3. People clapped their hands when the rocket (　　　　　　　　) as scheduled.
4. A team of alpinists (　　　　　　　　) their camp near the summit of the mountain last night.
5. The divers are attracted by the coral reefs (　　　　　　　　) colorful fish.

| build up in　　lift off　　set up　　teem with　　work out |
|---|

IN-DEPTH REVIEW

本文の内容に合うようにa～cから(　　)に適切な語(句)を選びましょう。

t 1

1. The Red Planet (　　　　).
   a. allowed humans to stay there
   b. is inaccessible to a spacecraft
   c. would require over one year for the astronauts' round-trip
2. A space trip to Mars (　　　　).
   a. would be free from any danger
   b. would present many risks to the health of the astronauts
   c. could affect the Earth's magnetic field

t 2

1. Mars explorers would be (　　　　).
   a. growing vegetables in the space station
   b. unable to bring many things with them to the planet
   c. creating tools for growing lettuce
2. Humans on Mars could (　　　　).
   a. destroy the environment of Mars by infecting it with microbes
   b. use carbon dioxide produced by NASA's Perseverance rover
   c. use their human microbes to find life on Mars

DL 45 CD2-77

## Summary

**以下の a ～ d を本文に出てきた順番に合うように並べ替え、それぞれの Part の要約文を作りましょう。最後に音声を聞いて確認しましょう。**

Part 1

a. One of the threats to astronauts is the existence of harmful cosmic rays, which can cause serious health problems.

b. Compared with a few days' trips to the moon, for example, it will take the astronauts much longer time to reach Mars.

c. Astronauts will have to cope with the health risks peculiar to space travel, such as weakened bones and muscles.

d. If human explorers successfully set foot on Mars, they could perform their tasks more effectively than robots.

Part 2

[ ] → [ ] → [ ] → [ ]

a. In addition to protecting the astronauts, we must take care not to pollute the existing environment of Mars with Earth's microbes, for example.

b. Unlike astronauts staying at the space station, Mars explorers must do without any supplies, such as food, equipment, etc., being restocked during the journey.

c. Constructing a colony on Mars and surviving there would pose far more difficulties to the explorers.

d. How to secure plenty of oxygen to breathe is another question, and scientists are planning to separate oxygen molecules from $CO_2$.

## Writing Strategy

**日本語の意味に合うように [　　] 内の語を並べ替え、英文を完成させましょう。**

1. 多額の寄付金はもとより、その NGO の救援物資は、とても大きな手助けとなった。

   The NGO's relief goods [ *help* / *no* / *small* / *were* ], [ *its* / *mention* / *not* / *to* ] large contributions.

   ______________________________

2. 我々が宇宙旅行をする場合は、必ず、地球の微生物を他の惑星へ放出しないことだ。

   If we make a space journey, we must [ *are* / *Earth's* / *ensure* / *microbes* / *not* / *on* / *released* / *that* ] other planets.

   ______________________________

## Clue to Usage

### No+形容詞

形容詞や副詞の前にnoが付くときは、大体はnot at allの意味で捉えてよい。But surviving this adventure would be no easy feat. (ℓ. 7)「しかしこの冒険を乗り切るのは生易しい芸当ではない」のno easyもnot at allの意味で捉えられる。ほかにも下記のような例文がある。

ex) It's a matter of no small importance. (= It's a matter of great importance.)
She explained it in no obscure words. (=She explained it in very clear words.)

### But then ... の読み取り

But then there's space radiation to worry about. (ℓ. 21) のBut then ... の表現は使い方が難しく、前後関係をよく見る必要がある。まずFor one thing, floating in microgravity for long periods weakens bones and muscles. (ℓ. 16) にて「1つには」という文が先にあって、無重力が骨や血流に及ぼす影響を述べている。それに対し、この文では「ただ、そのことで言えば」もしくは「ところで、それとは別に」といった流れで、別の問題点である宇宙線の害に話を移している。On one hand もしくはFor one thingと対照させた場合のOn the other handの意味だと考えるとよい。

ex) He gave no money to charity. But then I knew he was not the type to help others.
上の文では、チャリティーに寄付する、しないの是非からは論点を移して、「そういうタイプの人間ではない」と、別のコメントをつけている。

DL 46 CD2-78

## Approaching the Contents

**質問文の下線部分を書き取り、解答をa～dから選びましょう。**

1 **Q:** What is expected to ______________________________?

**a.** Keeping blood flow smooth.
**b.** Removing artificial gravity.
**c.** Taking necessary vitamins.
**d.** Weakening bones and muscles.

2 **Q:** What does the author think is key ____________________ of Mars?

**a.** Departing lightly equipped for safety's sake.
**b.** Taking care not to infect the planet with Earth's microbes.
**c.** Making sure that an oxygen factory is set up.
**d.** Compromising the scientific search for life.

# Over to you!

1～4は火星探査に関するFAQです。質問に対する回答を (a) ～ (d) から選びましょう。また、[　　] に適切な語を Keywords から探して英文を完成させましょう。

## FAQs

1. Does any life exist on Mars? (　　)
2. How can enough oxygen for the astronauts be secured? (　　)
3. Why is Mars called the Red Planet? (　　)
4. Have any rovers succeeded in landing on Mars? (　　)

## Answers

**Keywords** 1. device / 2. evidence / 3. orbit / 4. surface

(a) Mars is named after the war god Mars in Roman mythology. Most likely the reddish-orange color was associated with blood and fire in war. The fact is that the planet's desert-like [　　　　] is covered with dust that contains iron oxide, which gives it a rusty red color.

(b) H. G. Wells introduced the Martians in his novel *The War of the Worlds* as early as the 19th century. Of course, that was fiction. Today, NASA's Perseverance rover has collected samples of rock containing organic material that is a clue to indicate that life might have existed billions of years ago. Still, this is not definite [　　　　] of life on Mars.

(c) As Mars is our familiar neighbor, several nations have planned space missions to the planet, entering into an [　　　　] around it, landing on the surface, and running rovers. NASA has sent more than five rovers, including Curiosity and Perseverance. China also succeeded in landing its Mars rover.

(d) The thin Martian atmosphere is mostly composed of carbon dioxide. And NASA experimented with producing oxygen using a new [　　　　] called 'MOXIE.' It successfully split $CO_2$ and produced CO and $O_2$ separately. At the stage of the experiment, however, the quantity of obtained oxygen was very small and would not be 'enough' for future astronauts.

## Acknowledgements

### Text Credits

Unit 1 Night lights make even the seas bright
https://www.snexplores.org/article/light-pollution-sea-ocean-new-maps

Unit 2 Why teens can't help tuning out mom's voice
https://www.snexplores.org/article/mom-voice-kid-brain-teen-neuroscience

Unit 3 Let's learn about the future of smart clothing
https://www.snexplores.org/article/lets-learn-about-the-future-of-smart-clothing

Unit 4 Let's learn about Earth's secret stash of underground water
https://www.snexplores.org/article/lets-learn-about-earths-secret-stash-of-underground-water

Unit 5 Americans tend to see imaginary faces as male, not female
https://www.snexplores.org/article/faces-objects-imaginary-male-female-perception-pareidolia

Unit 6 This robotic finger is covered in living human skin
https://www.snexplores.org/article/robotic-finger-human-skin-self-healing

Unit 7 New meat-scented food flavoring comes from sugar — and mealworms
https://www.snexplores.org/article/mealworms-sugar-new-seasoning-smell-meat

Unit 8 Some deep-seafloor microbes are still alive after 100 million years!
https://www.snexplores.org/article/ancient-deep-seafloor-microbes-alive-after-100-million-years

Unit 9 Wildfires are pumping more pollution into U.S. skies
https://www.snexplores.org/article/analyze-this-wildfires-are-pumping-more-pollution-into-u-s-skies

Unit 10 News stories about spiders are unfairly negative
https://www.snexplores.org/article/spider-bite-misinformation-news-errors

Unit 11 Could a toothpaste help treat peanut allergy?
https://www.snexplores.org/article/experimental-peanut-allergy-toothpaste-treatment

Unit 12 NASA's DART spacecraft successfully bumped an asteroid onto a new path
https://www.snexplores.org/article/nasas-dart-spacecraft-successfully-bumped-an-asteroid-onto-a-new-path

Unit 13 What is sickle cell disease?
https://www.snexplores.org/article/explainer-what-is-sickle-cell-disease

Unit 14 Doppler effect
https://www.snexplores.org/article/scientists-say-doppler-effect

Unit 15 Let's learn about surviving a trip to Mars
https://www.snexplores.org/article/lets-learn-about-surviving-a-trip-to-mars

## Photo Credits

Unit 3 (p. 26)〔1980s〕©Ulf Wittrock | Dreamstime.com
〔1990s〕Steve Mann's wearable computer invention, Mann, Steve. "Smart clothing: The shift to wearable computing." Communications of the ACM 39, no. 8 (1996): 23-24, Mann, Steve. "Smart clothing: The wearable computer and wearcam." Personal Technologies 1 (1997): 21-27.
〔2010s〕©Razvan Nitoi | Dreamstime.com

Unit 4 (p. 29) ©Bgopal | Dreamstime.com

Unit 6 (p. 41, p. 43〔right, left〕) Shoji Takeuchi Research Group, The University of Tokyo

Unit 8 (p. 55) ©JAMSTEC

Unit 9 (p. 62) ©Shufu | Dreamstime.com

Unit 12 (p. 83) NASA, ESA, STSCI, HUBBLE (p. 85〔right, left〕) ASI, NASA

Unit 14 (p. 99) NASA'S IMAGINE THE UNIVERSE

本書にはCD（別売）があります

# Science Bridge

ニュースでつなぐ日常と科学

2024年１月20日　初版第１刷発行
2024年２月20日　初版第２刷発行

編著者　野﨑　嘉信
松本　和子
Alastair Graham-Marr

発行者　福岡　正人

発行所　株式会社　金星堂

（〒101-0051）東京都千代田区神田神保町 3-21
Tel　(03) 3263-3828（営業部）
(03) 3263-3997（編集部）
Fax　(03) 3263-0716
https://www.kinsei-do.co.jp

編集担当　稲葉真美香　Printed in Japan
印刷所・製本所／萩原印刷株式会社



ISBN978-4-7647-4203-1　C1082